MW01172725

BUILT

GOD TOUGH

An Anthology Presented By
Tee Hubbs

© 2023 Tee Hubbs

Book Cover Design: Antoinette Redji |Dr. Tamika Hall
Interior Book Design & Formatting: TamikaINK.com
Editor: TamikaINK.com

ALL RIGHTS RESERVED. No part of this book may be reproduced in any written, electronic, recording, or photocopying without written permission of the publisher or author. The exception would be in the case of brief quotations embodied in critical articles or reviews and pages where permission is specifically granted by the publisher or author.

LEGAL DISCLAIMER. Although the author has made every effort to ensure that the information in this book was correct at press time, the author does not assume hereby disclaim any liability to any party for loss, damage, or disruption caused by errors or missions, whether such errors or omissions result from negligence, accident, or any other cause.

Published By: TamikaINK

Library of Congress Cataloging-in-Publication Data has been applied for

ISBN: 9798851932939

PRINTED IN THE UNITED STATES OF AMERICA

Acknowledgments

This book is dedicated to YOU. Yes, YOU reading this. The Unshakable & the Unbreakable. You might sway but you won't break. You might get weak, but God will be made strong.

And to encourage, inspire and motivate women all over the world that no matter what you are going through, if God brought out these 30 women- surely He will do the same for you...

TABLE OF CONTENTS

FOREWORD

BY GEMIKA MOORE-POWELL

The walk with God, our faith, and this Christian journey aren't for the faint of heart. The trials we face, feelings of insecurity and inadequacy we endure, petitions we pray, and the breakthroughs that eventually come are designed to make us BUILT GOD TOUGH. What exactly does it mean to be Built God Tough? Let's allow James 1:2-4 to give us a preview of what it means. "Consider it pure joy, my brothers and sisters, whenever you face trials of many kinds, because you know that the testing of your faith produces perseverance. Let perseverance finish its work so that you may be mature and complete, not lacking anything."

Do you want to get deeper, real? We didn't quite make it to your block? Ok. The failed relationships that resulted in soul ties and resentment. The addictions that left you empty and broken. The children born out of wedlock or abortions manifested feelings of guilt. The secret lusts that imprisoned you into a cell of shame. The abuse, unexpected loss, or other trauma that engulfed you in feelings of bitterness and unworthiness and left you in pieces.

Now that I have your attention, let me assure you that God is intentional and has a purpose for all the pain, perceived setbacks, and even those times when you felt He was silent and didn't hear your prayers. Yet you found out He was still on the throne working things out. God Tough is a compilation of relatable life experiences and testimonies shared by women who have had their faith tested and came out on the other side to be an example to others about who God is and what He can do.

The women in Built God Tough are an example of what it looks like to be delivered from what the world said they were to who God has purposed them to be— REDEEMED. An example of what it means to walk out of seasons and chapters of life designed to steal, kill, and destroy—DELIVERED. They are the personification of what it looks like to rely solely on the Word of God when reality suggested they should give up—BLOOD BOUGHT. They are the epitome of what it means for you and me to be BUILT GOD TOUGH.

For many are called, but few are chosen.
-Matthew 22:14

-Gemika Moore-Powell

GEMIKA MOORE-POWELL

Gemika **Moore-Powell** is the founder and CEO of Walking In Purpose, LLC. With more than 16 years of business and change management experience gleaned through her career in national security, consulting, and tech industries, Gemika brings

9

a unique perspective to financial literacy. She stands on a platform to educate, inform, and inspire. Her passion and expertise are aligned with empowering people to walk in their purpose, transforming hearts and minds, and promoting growth by teaching biblical principles of stewardship.

For more information, visit:
www.walking-in-purpose.com or send an email to gemika@walking-in-purpose.com.

INTRODUCTION:

BUILT NOT TO BREAK

BY TEE HUBBS

I'm sure you have all heard about Murphy's law. Murphy's Law is an epigram that states "everything that could go wrong, will go wrong" and, in some cases, at the worst possible time. And, of course, meaning that in a negative sense. There was a time when Murphy, whoever he was, his law was getting the best of me. It seemed like everything that could possibly go wrong in my life did. Life was just life-ing and would not let up. It started throwing some serious punches that made me weaker and weaker day by day. The punches began to hurt so bad that I got tired of fighting back. I was fed up with life knocking me down. My solution was to end it all. I thought everything would be better if I forfeited the fight. "Dear Life, you don't have to knock me down anymore. I'm going to lay myself down and stay there." I thought. Those were my intentions when I consumed two bottles of 500 mg Tylenol and chased every pill two by two with Natural Ice beer until it felt like my throat locked up and I could no longer swallow. I went and laid in my bed and told God, "I better not wake up." I wrote a letter to my son, mom, and family, assuming that would be my last moment in this fighting ring called Life. I fell asleep and woke up five minutes later. I felt so sick, and no matter what I did or what position I laid in, I could not fall back asleep. Even when I wanted to lay there and give up, God's strength picked me up. I called one of my best friends at the time, and she took me to the hospital. They revived me and pumped my stomach by having me drink the most disgusting liquid that smelled like rotten eggs. Yuk. But God showed me at that moment that I still had the strength to carry on.

Evidently, life didn't get that same memo. When God put me back in the ring, now life was throwing body shots. I thought blows to the face hurt. But I soon learned that body shots are the ones that can really take you down. When I started losing everything, including myself, I really thought it was over. I remember looking in the mirror and not even recognizing who I was anymore. My face was sunken in, my hair was stringy and breaking off, my nails were brittle, my cuticles were bleeding from biting them, my eyes were yellow, and my skin had a cloudy pale darkness to it. My eyes were puffy from crying. That wasn't new; I cried every day.

"How did I get here?" I asked myself, staring at me in the mirror.

"Who are you?" I said with disappointment. I realized that I had lost everything. My heart was shattered into pieces from continuing to allow love to control me and not controlling it. And from giving love all that I had no matter what it cost. It cost me my family, my son, my identity, and my mind. All things that I gave up for a period of time, seeking after something that I had all along. But I could no longer stand the sight of me. I couldn't take one more relationship beating up. I was over the physical, mental, and emotional abuse. I was over going back and forth with my identity and being a lesbian. I was tired of addictions to love, attention, sleeping pills, parting, marijuana, and alcohol hovering over me and punching me until I lay there lifeless. The blows of disappointment from not being a good nurturing mother to my son at that moment were tearing me apart. The bruises of guilt from selfishly getting that abortion so that I didn't have to worry about another baby and be able to live my life were steadily knocking me down.

Depression and low self-esteem were kicking me in my gut. Oppression and discontentment were breaking my bones.

"Please stop!" I said to myself as I cried. This fight has to end! I had already attempted to settle this on my own four or so times before by trying to take my own life. I decided to go to God with a different approach this time.

Love took me to a new city and left me living in a one-room efficiency on one of the roughest streets in this city. I hated going in there. It smelled like urine, and there were drug addicts and dealers on every corner. I had just gotten my car back from repossession, thanks to my mother. I walked up the steps to unlock the door to my room with one motive. And that was to not come back out. I wanted to go to sleep and not wake up. I took a shower in the one bathroom provided for every room in that one house. I did my hair very nicely and got dressed up. I cleaned my whole room and wrote letters to my son, mom, and family. I laid down on my back in my bed as if I were lying in a casket.

I closed my eyes and said, "Dear God, I'm so tired. I hate it here. I hate my life. I don't want to be here anymore. Can you please take me with you? Please, God? I just want to be with you. I don't want to kill myself. I just want to be with you. Please take me." I remember slowly drifting off to sleep. And I had very high hopes of God answering that prayer.

It was the next morning. My eyes popped open like my body had been someplace else. I looked around with disappointment.

"I'm still here," I said, laying back down. I was still there. However, something was different. I felt different. The sun was shining through the one window in my room, and even it looked different. It was giving me life. "I haven't felt like this in a long time," I thought. I felt at peace. I laid there basking in that feeling for about 30 more minutes.

Then I heard a small still voice say, "Call your mom." I started to cry. I swallowed my pride and picked up the phone to call my mom.

"Hello?" she answered.

"Mom, can you come and pick me up?" I asked. "Of course! Where are you?" She replied. I could hear the joy and excitement in her voice. She and my son came to pick me up, and she took me "home." I felt like the prodigal daughter. I realized that God did answer my prayer. He didn't take me with him the way that I wanted. But He took control of the fight. I realized that everything that was happening wasn't happening to me, however it was happening for me. It was for my good and for the Glory of God. God was opening my eyes to see the light. He was just trying to get my attention. I kept trying to take control of the fight myself. But I can't fight with my own strength. Those things weren't really beating me up. I just had to let them go. I had to build my foundation on God. What is my foundation? My temple, mind, body, and soul. That is the only way I would be able to find the strength to stand up against the cares of life and this world. As God delivered me from each of those things above, I found strength and security that would last a lifetime and not for just a moment. It feels so good knowing that we do not have to worry about winning the fight because we serve a God that says, move, gimme that, I'll take it. I'll fight for you. And all we have to do is stand.

So, yea, I've heard of this "Murphy's Law." However, after all that I have been through, I know of God's Law! And His law says that "no weapon formed against me shall prosper," He is my refuge and my strength and a VERY PRESENT help. His law tells me to be strong and courageous and not fear...he will not leave me nor forsake me. His law says not to fear, He is my God, He is with me, and He will strengthen me, and He will help me and uphold me with his righteous hand.

And to cast my cares upon Him and that He will preserve me from trouble and surround me with shouts of deliverance.

My foundation is now solid. My foundation is now firm. My foundation is now Christ. I may sway, but I won't break. I may get weak, but God will always make me strong. I am Built God Tough. Period.

TEE HUBBS

Made in His Image, **Tamyra "Tee Hubbs" Hubbard** is just a chick out here who loves God and expresses that through being an author, Christian rap artist, liturgical dancer, poet, podcast host, and speaker. Tee uses creative speaking as an outlet to express her feelings and thoughts. Her two poems, She vs. Me and Scream, has been streamed all across the country. Over the years, she has invested in her first ministry, her only son, ensuring he stays on the right path with God. The investment in her son shaped her mission—encouraging, inspiring, and motivating women all over the world while leading those to Christ.

Tee is a Free Spirit with a slight quirkiness and enjoys being "The Weirdo." Tee is also a missionary that enjoys going into the trenches of third-world countries and helping to rebuild and spread the love of Jesus.

In 2021 Tee became a bestselling author after publishing her Creative Memoir book, SHE vs. ME: It Was the War Within for Me. Tee is also the producer of the stage play She vs Me, based on her memoir. She is also a co-author of International Bestselling anthologies, Courage to be Free, Momming & Queening, Letters to My Little Sister, and The Purpose in My Pain.

Her recent endeavors include releasing her most recent album, 40: Holy, which features her hit singles Crazy, God Tough, and Trouble in my way. And hosting the Holy Chicks Droppin' Nuggets Podcast with her best friend. Which is now streaming on all major platforms and has been streamed in 22 countries! So go pod up, subscribe, and listen y'all!

Tee boldly lives by "Stand for something or fall for anything." Tee stands strongly for her faith in Jesus. Her favorite scripture is Psalm 34:4. You can find

Tamyra "Tee Hubbs" Hubbard on the following social platforms listed below.

Contact/Booking info:
https://linktr.ee/TeeHubbs

IG: @tee_hubbs
FB: Tamyra Hubbard (TeeHubbs)
YouTube: Tee Hubbs
TikTok: Tee_Hubbs40
Website: www.teehubbs.com

Holy Chicks Droppin' Nuggets Podcast:
FB: holychicksdroppinnuggetspodcast
IG: holychicks_droppinnuggets
TikTok: holychicksdroppinnuggets
Link: https://holychicksdnpodcast.buzzsprout.com
Hey Siri & Alexa, "Play Holy Chicks Droppin' Nuggets Podcast!"

Subscribe to podcast:
https://www.buzzsprout.com/2015896/subscribe

Be a guest & booking info:
Email: holychicksdn@gmail.com

God, Please Don't Let Me Die

By Tocarra Derrickson

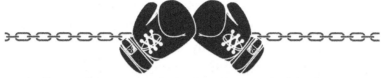

I dedicate this to my dad. Thank you, daddy, for being my coach, my support, and my biggest cheerleader.

I earned my "God Tough" badge on April 17, 2014. It was the day that God took away every piece of me. He took the brokenness, the hurt, the resentment, unforgiveness, the anger, the jealousy, the selfishness, the stubbornness, the alcoholism, the partying, the drinking, the fear of being alone, the sexual promiscuity, the guilt of abortion, the shame of having two failed marriages, adultery, and the biggest part of me—my voice and my humor. God used a moment of trauma to make me God Tough.

The Moment

It was a typical workday for me. After work, I came home and made plans to enjoy the rest of my day. It was the evening before Good Friday. Everyone was gone—just my youngest daughter and I were home. She was on the bottom floor, and I was upstairs in a room with one window that just so happened to be taped up because of my fear of stink bugs. Then it happened, the moment came–a fire broke out. We don't know how it happened, but it angrily started downstairs in the living room of our two-story rancher home. My daughter was playing on the computer in the backroom. Realizing a fire started, I managed to call my mother and 911. Finally, it was my moment to reap. It was as if that fire had a personal vendetta against me. It was as if it knew exactly where to find me, and it wasn't stopping until it took my last breath!

As black smoke filled my lungs, I felt myself leaving. It was time to give up, and I did. I covered my face and said, "God, please don't let me die." That was and still is my last memory of that day. Then came the time for the fire to do what it was designed and purposed to do. It started to consume an unconscious me by burning my scalp, neck, back, bottom, and hands. As I lay entrapped on that second floor while smoke and fire vented from the front of the home, I had no idea the battle being fought outside—the battle to save our lives. My youngest was stuck in the back room. She put a blanket in front of the door and placed her small hands on the window for someone to find her. Two officers found her; they found my baby! Not only did they find her, but they also rescued her by breaking the window and pulling her out to safety. Then she saved me, "My mommy is still in there." As the fire continued to engulf my family home, the mission to rescue me began. I was pulled out of the window the same way I was brought into the world—naked. They began to perform CPR, but it didn't seem like I wanted to return.

The Petition

"Tocarra! Breath!" yelled my resolute mother as the rescue team performed CPR on me, but I must've missed her cue because I didn't resume breathing. Finally, they loaded me up in the ambulance.

"TOCARRA! BREATHE! COME ON!" yelled my relentless older brother riding beside me in the ambulance. God must've heard him because I had taken a deep breath by the time we got to the hospital. Jesus brought me back! Later I learned the blood of Jesus had to bring me back several times–talking about a fight for my life! Still unconscious and unaware of what was happening, I arrived at the hospital and flew to Shock Trauma before making it to my final destination, Johns Hopkins Bayview Burn Center. Surrounded by family and friends, the petition for my life continued, and God wasn't giving up! Instead, He was working on saving my soul.

The Fight

Waking up in a coma, again, waking up in a coma is a moment I will never forget. Not being fully awake but awake enough to know that you aren't in a place of reality was very scary. I got so tired and didn't know if I would ever see reality again. The only piece of reality during that time was a voice—the voice of my dad. "Tocarra, Tocarra, it's daddy. Me and Gerald are here." I knew that voice. It brought me comfort. Whenever the dreams and visions while being in a coma got too much, it was like God knew and sent my dad into my room at that very moment to soothe me.

Because of my dad's voice, I fought out of that coma. It was hard, so hard. I just wanted sleep. I just wanted the dreams to stop. They weren't just any dreams. They were different aspects of my life that I didn't want to face; however, before I could be truly delivered, I had to face some things. And the only way I could face them was for God to show me myself. I dreamt of still being connected to my aborted child. I dreamt of being in lava and unable to get up. The lava represented hell. I dreamt of being on an endless road and unable to stop. That was my dead-end relationship filled with lust, hatred, and resentment. I just wanted it to stop.

"Ms. Derrickson, what day is it?" asked the nurse as I opened my eyes and took in my surroundings. I heard the hissing sounds of the ventilator and saw a whiteboard with the date and name of the nurse. It smelled like antiseptic—a little bitter with undertones of the artificial fragrance contained in soaps and cleaners. I had a metallic and salty taste in my mouth. I felt exhausted like I had been running for my life.

The day I found out what happened to me didn't break me. I wasn't even surprised. The things that almost broke me were being unable to see or touch my children. When I finally saw them, the fear in my youngest daughter's eyes when she looked at me and my oldest not being able to connect with me was too much to bear. Not being able to express myself by talking. Not being able to breathe on my own. Not being able to walk. Being showered with cold water. The feeling of my breath being taken away every time the nurses suctioned my tracheostomy. Being prepped for surgery and my bed being deflated to the point where my burnt flesh was flush with the rails. The pain was excruciating. It was as if my skin was slowly being pierced by a thousand nails. Not being able to scream because I was frustrated. People coming in, looking at me like I was a science project. Seeing that blank look on my middle brother's face, the look of weariness that sat on my mother, and not knowing when I would be back to normal. I didn't realize normal was never coming.

I am and will forever be marked by the fire. And today, I am ok with that. So many times, I felt like giving up in that hospital room. The first time I was removed from the vent, I didn't realize breathing could be so hard. The first time I had to sit in a chair to strengthen my muscles, I didn't realize that sitting in a chair could bring so much pain. Then the day of disappointment came, and even though I was fully aware of my limits by then, I still thought I could stand up on my two legs. I remember when the physical therapist came in and motioned to him that I wanted to stand up. He looked at me and said, "Ok, go ahead." Knowing that I could not, he told me to do it anyway. I tried, but my legs ignored the senses my brain was sending to stand up. I never even made it out of that chair. I felt helpless, defeated, and broken.

In came my dad, "Oh wow! Look at you sitting up." He was so ecstatic to see me sitting in a chair. He saw it as a major accomplishment. As a matter of fact, my dad saw everything as a major accomplishment— rather it was big or small. The day the trach was removed, and I said my first word, you would've thought we made it to heaven by the way my dad shouted. Soon, I had to look at things how he looked at them. "Let's see what God does today" was my daily morning speech. My dad, my cheerleader, never left my side.

Victim to Survivor

The woman that collapsed on that second floor died that day. No matter how hard I tried, she could never be resurrected. Even though it came with many challenges then and even now, I had to accept my new identity. I had to learn to live without the brokenness, the hurt, the resentment, unforgiveness, anger, jealousy, selfishness, stubbornness, alcoholism, partying, drinking, fear of being alone, sexual promiscuity, the guilt of having an abortion, the shame of having two failed marriages, and being an adulterer. I was now free. The first test I had to face in accepting this new me was the test of learning the definition of true beauty. Finally, being able to use the bathroom on my own in the rehabilitation center, I decided to look at myself in the full-body mirror. I turned around, and it looked like I had dinosaur skin on my back, my thighs looked like a checkerboard, skin was missing from my neck and turned into a huge mass—a keloid, my hair was shaved now, my hands looked like they had dirt piled on them, and a two to three-inch pink scar was on my scalp. I was so ugly. I felt ugly. There was a period of time when I stayed away from mirrors and always kept myself covered. I pretended it was for the protection of my skin when in reality, I was ashamed of what I looked like. The stares and sideways glances I was getting from the people I grew up with, the "omg, is that your mom" conversations with their peers I had to ignore when picking up my girls from school, and the constant reminder of what happened to me every time I undressed.

It was so hard. I was grateful to be alive. I just didn't understand why God had to leave me so ugly. Did He want me never to forget what happened? Did He want me never to find a mate? Yeah, He set me free, but were my looks now my punishment? Was it my Miriam and Aaron moment? No, it wasn't. God wanted me to understand that true beauty is a heart posture, and my wounds were His markings of grace given to a sinner. True beauty has nothing to do with looks. I began to accept and embrace me- ALL of me. What I once saw as ugly was now beautiful in my eyes. All it took was one sentence from someone who probably to this day doesn't realize the yoke that was destroyed just by them saying, "Don't hide your burns; they are your war wounds!" War wounds? I had been to war, and God was and will forever be the victor! I went through many tests, and today at this very moment, I am God Tough!

TOCARRA DERRICKSON

Tocarra **Derrickson** is a creative, resilient, patient, and devoted woman of God. She uses her life as a blueprint to enhance others. Tocarra has learned that every situation, rather good, bad, or ugly is an opportunity to express the Love of God. In 2018 she published a handbook, "A Guide to Salvation," which put her into the position of Youth Leader.

Despite the setbacks of the pandemic in 2020, she realized the "how to" piece was missing in the Body of Christ, so she created a blog to educate others on how to navigate through life while still standing for God. Fueled by the loss of her father, she developed a Machinima Patreon series which expanded her scope to a content creator. One thing that is consistent and unwavering in every circumstance—Tocarra is God's chosen.

Contact: Tocarra Derrickson
Email: Tderrickson3@gmail.com
Instagram: Tocarra_d1

You're Gonna Be Ok!
By Takiyah S. Turner-Barney

When you say "I do" before God, you take into consideration all of your vows to the highest level. For richer or for poorer, for better or for worse... 'til death do us part. I just didn't realize how powerful these words really were until I was faced with honoring them all.

On June 3, 2022, my **husband and** I decided to start a new life. We sold our home and bought a new one. He trusted me so much he didn't even see the house until we moved in. On July 3, 2022, exactly one month after, my whole world came crashing down, and my worst nightmare came true.

I witnessed my husband get murdered with just one shot to the head. I remember looking at him as soon as I heard the startling gunshot. That was the last time I saw my lifeless soul mate look me in the eyes before he fell to the ground. That image plays in my head every day. As I watched him fall in slow motion, I felt my whole body shut down. It literally felt like my spirit was removed from my body. So many emotions and conversations were replaying in my head at that moment. Even the words "It's gonna end today" which were the last words I heard him speak before the shot took place.

I had so many questions fluttering through my mind after this. Questions for God, myself, and others involved. Why? How? What could have been done differently? Is this even real?

"Feel free to wake me up anytime, God," I said.

A week later, I remember going into zombie mode. It was like I was on autopilot. As if I was existing, and not living. Sure, I've lost people to death before. Close people. But I have never felt this deep level of sadness before. It was a hard raw emotion. My emotions were all over the place. I was sad. I was mad. I was numb, lonely, and empty. Oh, and very vulnerable.

These emotions were different for me. I was used to being strong and tough for everybody else. I grew up as a military brat. My daddy raised me to be God Tough. Nothing broke me. I could shake it off and keep it moving. But this one hit different. This showed me a different perspective of what it meant to be *tough*.

Witnessing this changed me drastically. It changed me financially, mentally, emotionally, and physically. It's like I had to renew my vows with myself. The Takiyah that was before July 3 no longer exists. I now suffer from post-traumatic stress disorder (PTSD) and anxiety. My stress levels can also get high. I'm always looking over my shoulder and I sometimes have fear for my safety. I have been working with a therapist that has been very instrumental in giving me the tools and resources to deal with my up and down emotions.

I can sometimes hear that gunshot in my sleep. My appetite has not been good, and even sleeping has been a challenge. I didn't know how I was going to find the strength to go home to our new home every day and sleep in a bed without my husband. Remembering when we would lay in bed and joke about our day and have family calls (he loved himself some family calls).

God gave me such a peace in coming home. And those memories became a comfort to my soul. I laugh, and I cry. But I'm comforted.

At the time of writing this chapter, it's only been nine months since he was taken from me. So, I'm still on the road to forgiveness. In the process, I have learned a lot about myself. I've had to distance myself from negative people in order to heal and protect my peace. I've learned how important living in the moment is. I used to be on the go and always moving at a fast pace. Running around and trying to be everywhere for everybody. I don't rush anymore. I reevaluate things and life. And most importantly, I've learned how to say "no." There is such pleasure and peace in that one word. I'm calmer. I focus on the positive. Now, I can't even get mad anymore; not saying that I won't again. My spirit just does not allow me to feel that emotion.

Prayer, breathing techniques, and meditation have gotten me through these last few months. I now focus on me. And what's healthy for me. I'm finding out who I am. And not who I am for everyone else. But who God wants me to be for Him. There is such peace in living this way. I've learned that being tough means being at peace.

I thank God every day for my family, close friends, lawyer, motorcycle club and community for keeping me and my family in their prayers. I think of an old song, *"One day at a time sweet Jesus, that is all I'm asking of you. Just give me the strength to do every day what I have to do..."*

"Where are you today?" people ask. Well, after the sentencing of his murderer, I was totally out of it. I was weak. And I remember my cousin sitting beside me and just telling me to breathe as the judge was speaking the sentence. Now that that part is over, I'm slowly making my way back into the public. I actually want to be back out in front of people. I'm ok with talking about what happened without breaking all the way down. And I'm happy. I'm happy that I can stand before God and say that I truly honored every vow that I set before Him. And now, after my renewed vows with myself, I'm back to finding me. And I know that after making it through this, I'm gonna be ok.

Love on your loved ones. Hug them. Kiss them. Forgive them. Build relationships with them and friends. You never know when death will do you part. But if it does, let me be the first to tell you that "You're gonna be ok!"

My cousin Amber has been my rock through my journey! I'm grateful and thankful for my two children, Autumn and Cordell and my stepson, Eshan. I've lost a lot of family but through it all, God has kept me going, and I have a whole community behind me and all I can say is "THANK you!"

Lastly, I dedicate this chapter to my husband, the late George S. Barney III. I will continue to keep your legacy going. I AM BUILT GOD TOUGH!!

TAKIYAH S.
TURNER-BARNEY

Takiyah S. Turner-Barney **(Kiya)** is The Hype girl as most people know me by. I grew up a military brat. Traveling around to different states exposed me to different area's and I learned quickly to adjust to my environment. After my father left the military, we settled back in good ole Queen Anne's County Eastern Shore MD. Being a caregiver by nature, I then ventured into the hospitality field where I found my niche as a server for 19 years. When my mom fell ill, I was her caregiver. She soon passed on but told me that I would make a great nurse before she did. So, I went on to start my career at Comfort Keepers. My creative nature led me to become the owner and founder of Lucy's Girl's, LLC Day of event coordinators. I currently offer my supervision services as a breakfast supervisor at The Hyatt. I must say, I love my job! I pour my love into food and people. In 2015, I married the love of my life, George. We were married for 6 years.

In my free time I highly enjoy taking Xtreme hip hop step classes and dancing as a form of therapy. And if the music is lit, I can hype anyone up to dance. For this reason, I take much pleasure in coaching the UQA little league cheerleaders and the dance team at Queen Annes high school. I also take much joy in spending time with all of my children (birthed and by marriage) and my 5 grandchildren. And I love a good find at a flea market. Our Motorcycle Club, Homeboys BC/SC.

Takiyah_turner@yahoo.com
Facebook @TakiyahBarney
Instagram @Takiyah Barney
Snapchat @Takiyah Barney
Takiyahturner-barney.com
Tiktok @takiyahbarney

His Grace Is Sufficient
By Gwen Edwards

Here I go again, second marriage, third child, a marriage that I thought was built with love, communication, and friendship. We both love music and writing; we have the same belief in discipline and morals; it seemed perfect. I converted to Islam, and that is when it all changed. He had a hobby of roller skating, something I never minded, he began staying out three to four nights a week, and he got new friends, none that I would ever meet; shortly after the belittlement followed, the disrespect came to the nude pictures in his digital camera on his weekend getaway, the phone calls the text messages from the other women. I didn't work outside the home, it was his idea, I was a stay-at-home wife and mother, and I enjoyed that.

Our baby boy, one-year-old, things had really gotten bad at this time. He was never home. One night, he came home from hanging out with his friends he walked up the stairs, I was in the bathroom on my knees painting the woodwork, I looked up, as he looks down.

His eyes had hate in them, his lips twisted up, and his nostril was flared, and he said, "What are you doing?"

With a nasty tone, I replied, "Painting."

He looked like he wanted to just kick me in my face, but he walked away. At that point, I knew he hated me. I knew there was someone else that stole his heart, and he wanted me gone; my heart dropped, and I stayed in the bathroom silently praying to God to help me.

The mental abuse continued, and I was walking around on eggshells, I made sure the house was clean and organized and food was cooked just to keep him quiet. The kids were afraid to move around the house freely. His voice would rattle the walls, and I thought to myself, "I have nowhere to go" and I didn't want to tell my mother and sister that they were right. They told me not to give up my independence and not to give up my house, but I trusted him 100% and allowed him to lead.

I was renting a house, but I gave everything up to move into his house because his house was paid off and it seemed like a good idea financially; besides, we are married. Big mistake. He would tell me often, "You have nothing. If you leave, you have nowhere to go, and no man wants a woman with three kids."

I would cry and pray to God to help me. I felt like nothing! My self-esteem was so low. I thought to myself, "What did I do for this man to hate me like this?"

I would talk to him and ask him can we work on this marriage, and can we spend some time together;

can I have one day a week with you, and maybe we can find a hobby like bowling. He seemed sincere, and he agreed, but he always let me down and would go out with his newfound friends.

One evening his son and I, who had just turned three years old, drove to his property. We were fixing it up to rent out, I had just finished having dinner with my mom, and the house was right around the corner, so I decided to see how he was coming along with the house. I knocked on the door. He was taking a very long time to answer. He finally opened the door and the look in his eyes was fear. I began to look confused myself, so I asked, "Who is in here?"

He replied, "No one."

I said, "Something is not right," so I started yelling out in the house. "Whoever is in here, show yourself now."

I walked all the way through the house in each room, and when I got to the last room, he yelled up the steps in a weird tone as if he was afraid, and said, "Gwen! Stop playing there's no one here!"

When he said that, the woman stuck her head out from behind the bedroom door, and I asked her, "What are you doing here?"

She replied, "He let me in."

I repeated my question, "What are you doing here? With my husband?"

She said, "He let me in!" With a shaky voice.

So, I said, "So, you don't know his name?"

She said, "Yes, but I was only here looking for a house for my mother."

I responded, "At this time of night, all the lights don't work in this house."

Then she said something really odd; she looked at me and said, "Wow! You're pretty, I'm sorry, Gwen."

I said, "So, you know my name?

She said, "Yes, your husband and I are just friends; besides, I'm married."

I looked at my husband and said, "So, this is what you have been doing?"

I said, "I'm going to take our son home, I'm done here, y'all two can go back to doing what y'all was doing," and I left.

I was crushed, but I had to stay strong for my boys, I had nowhere to go, and the mental abuse continued, I went to the Iman a couple of times for help; the last time they called him on the phone, and the way my husband was responding to the Iman, the Iman told me to take your kids and leave him, it doesn't sound like he is going to change. One time he got so tired of me being there that he kept asking randomly, "When are you leaving?"

I kept telling him I needed help, and I had no money; he grabbed my wrist and tried to pull me down the stairs to throw me out of the house; I was holding on to the banister, the kids were crying, and he finally let me go. I grabbed the boys and told them that I was sorry that they had to witness that, and I will get us out of there, and that will never happen again. My mother and sister talked to my husband and said to him "Since you want her to leave, can you allow her and the kids to move into your other house until she gets on her feet?" He replied, "NO, does she got rent money? She will pay like anybody else."

Shortly after I got a job, and I would take my son to a Christian daycare center. Every day this owner would just pour into me; she would read scripture from the bible to me, and she would pray over me as I left out to go to work. She shared with me intimate stories of her marriage and she would give me life stories of things that happened to her and the things her husband did to her. And how she had to stay strong for her kids. She just worked, went to school and prayed every day, and God changed her life.

I shared with her what I was going through at home, she would pray with me, and she would tell me all these wonderful things about God and Jesus and about his love. I had always known there was a God, but I was always afraid of him, I was always raised to believe that my mother was my first God and that if I did something wrong, even the littlest thing, God was going to get me like the boogie man. I honestly did not know God loved me unconditionally. One evening my sister was taken back to the hospital for some previous stomach pains from the day before that had gotten worst. I was headed back down to see her, and as I was getting dressed, my husband kept following me around the house, tormenting me, repeating, "Why don't you just leave! Go back to your mother's house."

I told him, "I wasn't in my mother's house when you married me."

I walked into each room to get away from the emotional abuse, but he kept following me. I walked back into the bedroom, and he just kept tormenting me about how much he wanted me out of his life.

He said to me, "You are the reason why she got an abortion!" He said it with such conviction!

He blamed me for his mistress choosing to have an abortion. I stopped, turned around and looked at him. I couldn't breathe, I couldn't speak. A tear dropped, my heart dropped, I felt numb, then I felt weak, my phone rang it was my niece telling me my sister died. He could hear my niece crying through the phone. I started screaming, and he looked at me, and he said, "I'm sorry, I'm sorry, I didn't mean anything I just said, just forget about it all."

It was already too late. I heard everything he said. But I couldn't respond, my only sister was dead, I must get to my mother, was my only thought. He went back to his ways after the funeral; his mistress, the one who was hiding in the house, left her husband for my husband; she still felt threatened by me, so she would make up lies about me, such as, she would put a hard piece of candy in her gas tank, but not small enough that it would fall in the gas line, then she would tell him, "Your wife is putting candy in my car trying to destroy my car."

So, he would believe her and curse me out. Then she had someone throw eggs on her car and had someone say they saw me do it, and he believed her again and cursed me out. I would try to reason with him and have him think about how stupid it sounded, I would say, "Think about it!"

This woman broke up my marriage and destroyed my family, and all I did was throw eggs on her car, and that would cost $3.99 for a car wash and a piece of candy in her gas tank that you were able to pull out with your finger. I said if I wanted to destroy her car, I would have put sugar in the gas tank, and I wouldn't have thrown eggs. I have three kids to feed. And I would have flattened three of her tires and then broke out the back window. But he believes everything this woman said. She had his heart and mind, and I lost. I was still taking my son to the daycare center, and the owner was still pouring into me about God's love.

I broke down crying, I hated myself, I hated my life, and I contemplated suicide; she went into her file cabinet and said, "Here are the keys to my house; this is the address; you don't have to go through this anymore, take the kids and leave. I have not been there in a while, but there should be some towels and sheets in the house for you to use. We will work out details later." I got in the car; my heart was racing, the tears were flowing, and I was in complete shock that someone would help me, I was screaming JESUS, JESUS, JESUS!

I tried to keep it a secret from him until I got everything together, but he found out once the gas company called my phone, confirming my turn-on date. He was shocked to find out I was moving. He said, "You can't afford anything; how did you get a house? Are you moving with some man?"

I said, "No." I would never do that again.

So, I moved into my house; it needed a lot of work, it was empty for a while. There was water damage and the mice were taking over, but I didn't care, it was peaceful, and my brother came through and helped me out a lot. There were times when I had no food, and I was too prideful to ask my mother or brother, I knew they would have given it to me, I just felt stupid for giving everything up to marry him. One evening I asked him for $50.00 because we had no food, and I wasn't qualified for any government assistance.

He said he would. I called him several times after, but he never showed up. I ended up going to the salvation army for a bag of food to feed the kids, I remember like it was yesterday. It was a bag of frozen fried chicken, a few cans of fruit, a bag of rice, peanut butter, milk and canned goods.

My oldest son was always getting in trouble, ditching school; after multiple programs failed to work, the judge placed him in a residential facility, and the state sued me for Child Support. Things really got hard; I began to really dig into the word of God. I began feeling different, like stuff was happening around me, and I wasn't responding the way that I normally would; I was beginning to feel God's presence and hear his voice inside of me. One night I was asleep, and something kept pulling me out the bed and I kept running back in the middle of the bed. The voice was telling me to get up. Someone is vandalizing your car. And I could see the person in my dream. It was a woman and a young man, scratching and kicking it.

When I woke up the next day, I went outside, and my car was badly damaged. I called up my husband, and I told him, "You told her where I lived, and she damaged my car!" He didn't believe anything I said. He just said she would never do that. That's when I filed the divorce papers and restraining order. I was done! It was a blessing that she vandalized my car, I received a check from my insurance company, I got the car fixed, paid bills, and brought groceries.

Once I began to know God, his love for me and his plan for me, and I forgave my husband for the way he treated me, I felt like I was on cloud nine. Nobody understood me. They said, "How could you talk to him after the way he treated you?" I kept telling people I am happy; my life is Good and God is Good. I had very little, but everything at the same time. I realized that all I needed was Jesus. My ex-husband has since apologized for his behavior; he says he should have never allowed the outside noise to get in. We are great friends today. The word of God says to be kind and compassionate to one another and to forgive each other just as Christ God forgave you. (Ephesians 4:32)

Fast forwarding four years later, I meet my now husband at church, I know it's cliché, right, lol. This man prays over me while I sleep; it used to disturb me at first; before I realized what he was doing. All I would hear was a bunch of mumbling. Lol. He rubs my feet and back every night, he still brings me flowers once a month, and eight years later, he still tells me I'm beautiful. And every single day, he says "Did I tell you I love you today?" And I'm like yes, an hour ago. Then he says well I don't remember and he will say it again. Lol. It's hard to separate the Good and the Bad times that I endured; it all went together for his glory; I'm blessed that God used the Day Care owner to strengthen my faith and guide me through some tough seasons. Jeremiah 29:11 says, "For I know the plans that I have for you, declare the lord, plans to prosper you and not to harm you, plans to give you hope and a future." God kept his promise.

GWEN EDWARDS

My name is **Gwen Edwards-Davis.** I'm a wife and mother of three boys and several grandchildren. I'm a Certified Medical Biller and Coder for 18 years. I received my education from

Walden University in HealthCare Management, I have been in the healthcare field for 25 years and held several leadership roles.

I have an online ministry called "Women by the Well Ministry." I also invest in Residential Real Estate; in other words, I'm a landlord. I'm never comfortable talking about myself and I do not like titles; I am not impressed by the position, status, and ranks. The position that I like to go by is that I am a servant of Christ.

When I'm not working, my 9-5, you can catch me doing biblical counseling, decorating my home, cooking, writing poetry, and reading books. My favorite authors are John C Maxwell, Myles Munroe and Zig Ziglar. I am the Matriarch of the family, so it's never a dull moment. Some people say I missed my calling as a comedian; I have a sarcastic humor; I love to laugh. I love the snow; my favorite season is winter, and I love the winter holidays. It's the time of the year when family comes together to share food and laughter.

It Was All a Dream

By Rahnice Parker

It was all a dream... well, so I thought. At least for those two weeks while my mind pondered on the details of what would inevitably become my reality. Did I say dream? Because to me, this was more like an out-of-body experience, something that felt so real but was almost impossible to believe. I can recall waking up from this dream, heart racing, sweating like crazy, feeling afraid, and very anxious all at the same time. It was about 2 am when I picked up the phone and called my friend to share; a lump of fear crept up in my throat as I attempted to blurt out what I had just experienced. Once I was able to get it out, I was too shaken up to fall back asleep. I couldn't sleep, drive, or think clearly for days. This would be the beginning of what I considered some of my life's darkest days.

February 24th has always been significant as it represents the birthdate of my twin brother and sister. Unfortunately, on February 24, 2009, at the young age of 27 years old, my life was changed forever. In the evening, my son (who was eight years old at the time) and I were getting picked up from Step Team practice that was being held at the church I was attending. The youth at the church were preparing to perform at a local conference they attended annually. I distinctly remember "God in Me" by Mary Mary playing as we were getting ready to leave the house and get into the van, greeted with warm, welcoming hellos from the children and adults that were already inside.

The ride from my house to the church is a trip that I will always remember; it was full of laughter and innocent adolescent conversations that were sensible but very much naïve in nature. The type of conversations about boys and friendships that made me giggle like a school-aged girl and left me feeling all warm and fuzzy on the inside. As we arrived at the church, the kids went inside and practiced like they normally would, only there was something special about the practice that night.

The unity and genuine love felt that night is unmatched. Watching the kids practice, laugh, and act silly, brought so much joy to my heart; it was refreshing to see. As practice ended, we loaded the van to head home. I got into the front passenger seat, and we started down the highway to drop everyone off at home. The ride home was not as exciting; you could vaguely hear conversations and music from the radio playing as I picked up my cell phone to make a call.

After hanging up, I sat back in the seat and closed my eyes, only to be startled by a loud BOOM! The impact was so strong that it caused the van to spin out of control; unable to make sense of what was happening, I did the only thing I knew how to do, I called on Jesus. The van, at this point, began to turn over multiple times. The sound of high-pitched screams could be heard over my own voice as we endured what felt like the scariest rollercoaster ride of my life. After what seemed to be a lifetime, we finally came to a halt, and everything became pitch black and fell silent. EVERYTHING!

I remember waking up in what looked like a maze; "God, where am I, and what just happened"? Those were my exact thoughts. As I attempted to get up and turn around, I realized that the van had landed on the right side, my side. Adrenaline pumping, I located the window and mustered up enough strength to break the remainder of the glass and jump out of the window. Not even realizing the damage that occurred to my elbow and the glass that cut my hands. I was more concerned about what needed to be done.

The next few moments consisted of a dreadful reality for myself and everyone else involved. I remember feeling terrified, wanting to run down the highway screaming and crying, but I snapped back into reality when I heard a voice say, "Mom," I'm sleepy. I turned around, and there stood my son. I had forgotten that he was even in the van; my mind was so confused. He had shards of glass in the right side of his head, and he was bleeding; I took off my sweatshirt and wrapped it around his head as a quick remedy and continued to assist my friend with locating and gathering all of the children. Standing in the middle of Rt 13 with tears streaming down my face, most of the children and myself cried out to the Lord, yelling "Jesus" at the top of our lungs. We were so desperate for help, and that was all we knew to do. I felt helpless. I have never felt more helpless in my life than I did at that moment.

A gentleman I knew from childhood saw the crash and stopped to see if we needed help. I used his phone to call my then Pastor and inform her that we had been in a really bad crash and that she needed to get there as soon as possible.

The next day, I slept for about an hour when the sun came up. Trying to make sense of everything that occurred, I thought to myself, was this a dream? As I turned on the news later that morning, it confirmed what I had been told at the hospital the night before. Two of the children, both girls ages 10 and 12, did not survive the crash that I was involved in. My babies? I strongly recall feeling distraught; I was so heartbroken and confused. A hurt that I could not even begin to put into words. Then there were instant feelings of guilt; how could I come home with my son, and these two mothers could not bring their babies home?

It was this day that I discovered Then/Now. Because life as I once knew it would never be the same. I literally felt like I wanted to crawl under a rock and DIE! I let them down. I had one job to do, and I could not protect them. How could I go on in life knowing that I could not stop this from happening? These feelings began to overtake me and did so for some time. Even though I knew God, believed in Him and trusted that His word was true, I did not feel like an overcomer; I felt defeated. Days went by, and eventually, I had to say my goodbyes to the girls.

We had their services together because it was too much of a heartache to even think about having two services to attend. The impact was so huge and affected everyone connected to me, so much so that it felt like I had very little support. Everyone was going through it. Although I knew that there were so many praying for all of us, I felt so alone and afraid. Weeks went by, and I still felt as though I was walking around in a daze, fake smiling (if at all) and crying daily behind closed doors. I continued to press my way to church and pretend as if things were getting better, but deep down inside; I was depressed and drowning in pain. This tragedy affected everything about my life; I couldn't be there for my son like I wanted to be because of the grief. He did not want to speak about it, and I did not know how to even get help for him. It took away my ability to be happy and my desire to live; I felt as if I was only existing.

Months went by, and while I stood in front of the church singing praise and worship, I was still making myself believe that Kayla and Tashaun would come running through the doors of the church, smiling, and letting us know that they were fine. It was just so much easier to trick my mind into believing that they were away and "ok" than to accept that two children I had grown to love as my family would never return to this life. Talk about being devastated! I ended up following the legal proceedings, and the man that was responsible for all the turmoil taking place in my life was found guilty of vehicular manslaughter and sentenced accordingly. This still did not take away the constant pain and grief that I experienced daily; it still was not bringing back the girls or taking away the trauma that I had endured because of his irresponsible decision.

A year or two went by, and I was connected to a lady that runs a Victim Impact Program by Renea, the mother of Kayla (the 12-year-old). After hearing about the program, I agreed to meet with the lady in hopes that I could find some sense of relief, closure, or healing. Walking around, feeling as though something inside of me had died, was taking a toll on my life, mentally, emotionally, and spiritually. I met with Mrs. Book to do a face-to-face and to get an understanding of how the program works and to allow her to hear my story. Let me tell you; I cried for almost an hour straight! All of those pinned-up emotions, all the anguish and pain, the fear of "telling it all" because I wanted to protect my loved ones from the details of that tragic night.

It was through Mrs. Book that I learned that I had been living with Survivor's Remorse/Guilt. I had almost become obsessed with the incident and the losses that occurred, causing constant feelings of helplessness, lack of motivation to move forward in life, and it just paralyzed me mentally. God had placed this woman in my life who had also experienced a great loss to help me navigate my healing process. I started volunteering at the local prison to share my story with those that were incarcerated, and it allowed me to openly express the forgiveness that God required me to extend to a person that changed my entire life forever. The outpour of love and self-reflection from the men and women that were incarcerated and heard my story was overwhelmingly reassuring and compelled me to continue my journey of healing.

Throughout my healing process, God has strategically placed people in my life to uplift, encourage, carry, and pour into me. Some strangers, and others that are near and dear to my heart. Two of those people happened to be the mothers of those two beautiful young girls; they have exhibited such strength and grace and extended it to me as well. Two others were the friends, Tonekia and Crystal, that endured this tragedy with me. Heartfelt conversations that involved both laughter and tears have played a significant part in my healing as well. Support and help have come in many forms, but God began working on my heart and mind by sending his word to be a comforter and sustain me. Renewing my mind and allowing me to stand when I really felt like lying down and dying.

Through the connection of Mrs. Book, I was introduced to my therapist... Yes, therapy and Jesus are a great recipe for healing! Baby, let me tell you that she is the bomb! And yes, she is a God-fearing Christian. I met her in December 2018, when things were not as bad, but grief and heartache and taken up residence in my life for nine long years. Between prayer, worship, and our therapy sessions, God took me further into my healing journey. This was necessary for me to share with others so that I would be equipped for what was to come.

Therapy has taught me and is still teaching me how to cope with PTSD, the anxiety and fear that sometimes shows up as a result of the trauma that I have experienced, how to fight against depression and thoughts that try to cripple my mind and control my daily activities. God has come into many of our therapy sessions and allowed true deliverance, healing, and freedom to break forth. Although the pain will never completely go away, and I still think about that night, the girls, and how it has affected me, I am grateful that God kept me and I made it this far, only by His grace and mercy. God pulled me out of that dark place, and He has set me on the path to healing and wholeness. He heard my cry, rescued me, and continues to rescue me. He built me strong and resilient. He built me tough... God Tough!

RAHNICE PARKER

Rahnice Parker was born in Providence, Rhode Island, and later moved to Bridgeville, Delaware, with her parents and siblings. She was raised most of her childhood in Delaware and then moved to a small town in Maryland by the name of Federalsburg. She now resides in Bridgeville, DE. Rahnice is the mother of a 23-year-old son and GiGi to a 3-year-old grandson she absolutely adores and finds great joy in spending time with. Rahnice is a God-fearing woman that stands firmly on the principles of grace and favor. She works as a Program Coordinator for an agency that provides care for individuals with disabilities (by way of occupation) but is ultimately a servant at heart. She is making her debut in this Anthology, "Built God Tough," but looks forward to introducing the world to her up-and-coming projects. The Best is yet to come!

Stay Tuned!

Seeking Self...

By Tonya Johnson

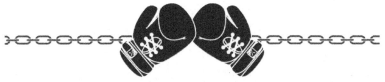

I have experienced many things in my life; hurtful downs, middles, and the immense ups—hurdle after hurdle after hurdle. The unfettering of them all was knowing that I was abiding daily under the wings of the Almighty. I was so very thankful for that grace. I say grace because I knew that God had granted me **His** unmerited favor! Nevertheless, here is where I had to become very aware of myself and what I was doing, thinking, and projecting, which is the stuff that matters. I was not living in my power, my next-level self.

The "self" that is very aware that the Word of God goes beyond just Sundays or walking with the Word only when I felt like it. I could do and say what I wanted because...well, just because. I was not living in peace, wisdom, authority, or obedience. Yet, I rested under His wings...how very selfish was I.

"He shall cover thee with his feathers, and under his wings shalt thou trust: His truth shall be thy shield and buckler" Psalm 91:4

I was in search of something, and something was looking for me too!

In my life, I never really felt true love before. I was desperate to feel a deep, fulfilling, unyielding love not just for a man or family bonds but for myself. My deepest desire was to own my next. My next level self. I knew I could achieve what I desired, but my belief was weak. I needed to feel that kind of love for myself. See, my life had begun to spiral out of control; I felt invisible, unheard, lost, and so alone. I was in search of *me* and who I truly was. Did I want to continue to be that woman? The woman who was unfulfilled, ravished in fear, stuck? Crying in the dark, asking when will it change? Feeling helpless.

When will I live the life, I had dreamed about? The fruitful life I believed God had created just for me....

This question was swirling around in my head. Who did I need to become? The feeling was deep in my belly... I felt it so strongly. I had been feeling a pull. *I* **knew who it was.** The feeling I was experiencing was not a what is that type of feeling? It was the *Holy Spirit*. The *Holy Spirit* is a gift that God left to all believers, and he indwells within us. He has all the power of God and will help us in every area of our daily living. To live in freedom and power, you must accelerate your belief and faith. I did! And it was inconceivably worth it!

Jesus said unto him, if thou canst believe, all things are possible to him that believeth.
Mark 9:23

I am here because I want to bring forth a transformation within you and walk with you into your freedom. Your power! Tap into the inner depths of you and know who you are. It's beyond Sunday!!! It's beyond going to church, sitting in the pews listening to the sermons, writing them down, and never applying it to our lives but knowing that we have a calling to fulfill - our purpose, and it is going to take some work. And that is ok!

I was living in lack and limitation in every area; my mind, my attitude, my behavior, and my results out of life. I remember a time when I couldn't even afford paper towels or toilet paper, surviving off peanut butter and jelly sandwiches and raisin bran cereal. Whooooo...If I could afford to go to the grocery store and pick up those limited items, oh man (and I can't forget about my cheese slices to snack on), I was doing good because having them was better than not eating at all.

I was aiming to make sound decisions, with so many to make at 19; I had yet to learn what I was doing, how to pay my bills, or how to take good care of a car. I was terrified at night to go to sleep. The enemy knew my fears, and he was pulling on every one of them. He was trying to take me out; he was trying to take my mind from me. He wanted me out of the game of life, BUT what he did not realize was that there was a warrior in me, and she was waking up. Because the good word is true; **"train up a child in the way he should go, and when he is old, he will not depart from it" (Proverbs 22:6)**. So, that training was wailing up in me.

Conversely, the enemy was also whispering in my ear, saying, "It's over! Nobody loves you; nobody likes you; you are not going to make it, girl. You're not worth the time. You won't survive. Why don't you just drive off the bridge into that ditch over there? Nobody will care. Nobody will miss you. Nobody will even look for you. You are not worthy; look at your mess!"

What he did not know was that I was remembering when I was abiding under the wings of God. Yes, in my mess *WITH ALL MY FLAWS*. God had me, and I believed He loved me even if I couldn't feel it right then. I started to reflect even in all my sadness and tears. I remembered what the Word of the Lord said about me. Not what other people may or may not have valued in me. I didn't know how, but I was going to make it. I was going to LIVE! And I am here to tell you; you are too! No matter what it is, you will make it with God.

I believed that even though I had been knocked down so many times, I could get back up! You must believe that same thing. I HAD to get back up, and now it is your time to get back up and get back to your God-given dreams. I knew I couldn't just live life in mediocrity! The *Word of God* told me I had greatness and power inside of me and that I believed! God did not need to give it to me; I realized I already had it. And guess what? He does not need to give it to you either....

YOU already have it too! Right now, you have it! Trust in the Holy Spirit: His guidance.

I decided to go all in with the Holy Spirit. Do you believe that there is greatness and power within you?

In one of my weakest moments, I fell on my knees and cried out to Him to help me; to pull out of me what He had already put in me. To trust Him fully! Guess what? He did! He did it, and I experienced the deepest, unending, unconditional, unyielding love that I desired. His unweaving strength and power. In Him, everything is possible. Your renewal, power, healing, and restoration. YOUR FREEDOM! Your freedom to be the unlimited, most successful you. Is anything too hard for God? No.

Ah, Lord GOD! Behold, thou hast made the heaven and the earth by thy great power and stretched out arm, and there is nothing too hard for thee - Jeremiah 32:17

Life has taught me, as a believer, that you can live in freedom, and you still must go through your valleys. Why? Because you must know and believe that you already have the victory! You win. Living consciously aware of the *Holy Spirit* and depending on His infinite power will enable you to overcome your struggles, strongholds, and adversities. It is the **omnipotence of God**! There is nothing He cannot do! And nothing he will not do for His child. He is all powerful, so you are all powerful. We can choose to tell the enemy to shut up and go! Surrendering ourselves fully to God. If you are not connected to God, now is the time!

As a father shows compassion to his children, so the LORD shows compassion to those who fear him. Psalm 103:13

See, that's why I'm so passionate about what I do....to share with you what I learned from overcoming the sadness, disappointments, pain, struggle, and adversities of this life, for they are great treasures. Look there, right there, and you will find your purpose! Right, there is where you can walk into your calling and live the highest version of yourself. To accept your life of joy, success, and victory! Become immensely aware of who you need to become and live in that version every day; you are the expression of your creation!

Troubles come to make us strong. Why? Because we are in training. Just because we are His children, that doesn't exempt us from the training. The crushing is necessary because once we get through it, again are the great treasures; our character is developed to be more like Jesus. We should always be in pursuit of being like Jesus. The pursuit doesn't have to be complicated; you must get to moving! Start, and it starts in your mind with a faithful decision! Strongholds, adversities, and struggles only have as much authority as you allow them to have in your life!

They shall come, but they are not your end! But you must choose that they are not your end!

For God has not given us a spirit of fear, but of power and of love and of a sound mind. Timothy 1:7

Some of the hardest lessons to learn are those we don't want to face or do not want to fully hear, accept, or let go of. Struggles don't have to be the end! Adversity doesn't have to be the end! Strongholds don't have to be the end. Face them; then, you can change them.

You can change the experience by changing the thought around the experience. Thoughts are powerful, and it is up to you to accept them or reject them. Immediately reject negative or bad and intrusive thoughts, whether they are new thoughts or thoughts of your past.

Begin to stand on God's truths. They are life-changing! Listen to that voice inside of you, pay attention to the signs, and listen to your intuition. ... what is God saying? What is he speaking to you? Begin to allow yourself to be open because you matter. God cares! He desires for you to live powerfully and in abundance! Say to yourself out loud, "I matter!"

Make it a declaration if you need to. Get to work because your triumphant life is waiting on you! I cannot stress this enough!

Now, I know that some of you may be feeling like you have lost so much time. You may think it is too late to start a business, get married, go back to school, etc. You think procrastination has stolen your dreams, and time is up. Well, I used to feel that way too, but again I am your evidence to the power of God. It is not too late. Start again! Seek him and ask him; he will restore to you the years! Yes, He will.

And I will restore to you the years that the locust hath eaten, the cankerworm, and the caterpillar, and the palmerworm, my great army which I sent among you.
Joel 2:25

Ask again! Start again. Know who you are...

Quote:

"True transformation is to be changed by the renewing of the mind; it's not conforming to the struggle, strongholds, and adversities."
~Tonya Johnson

Here are **three powerful truths** for you to ponder today and every day as you begin the process. There is a phenomenal amount of value in the *Word of God*. Make time to read and study. This will help you build a stronger relationship with God.

Remember, it is beyond Sunday! It is for every day.

1. God's Word is operative, working, and alive.

"All Scripture is breathed out by God and profitable for teaching, for reproof, for correction, and for training in righteousness.

2 Timothy 3:16

2. God's Word is revealing.
But, as it is written, "What no eye has seen, nor ear heard, nor the heart of man imagined,
what God has prepared for those who love him."

1 Corinthians 2:9

3. God's Word is life-giving.
"A thief is only there to steal and kill and destroy. I came so they can have real and eternal life, more and better life than they ever dreamed of.

John 10:10

TONYA JOHNSON

Tonya Johnson is the Founder and CEO of Perfecting Spirit & Mind Ministries, where they are stirring up the world! She declares, "you can live a life of fulfillment and triumph no matter what you have been through".

Tonya passionately loves inspiring and leading kingdom women to overcome struggle, strongholds, and adversity by being "renewed in the spirit and attitude" of your mind using biblical and kingdom principles. She is walking in her calling; fearlessly dedicated to helping women who feel stuck, broken, defeated, and scared; smash through restricting patterns, limited thinking, and behaviors to strengthen their faith and belief and facilitate with them; how to move forward in a powerful way!

Tonya is a 3x best-selling international author, inspirational & empowerment speaker, podcaster, and mentor/spiritual teacher. She is a Certified Christian Counselor and Certified Master Mindset & Meditation Coach. She holds a Master's Degree in Management with a specialization in HRM.

Tonya is a firm believer that we should always be learning, seeking understanding, wisdom, renewal, and awareness!

Tonya wrote her first best-selling book, "Overcoming Me," as evidence that "ALL things are possible" if you believe and have steadfast faith. The powerful book is an inspirational memoir that shares some of her life's journeys and the 10 dynamic principles she used to overcome past pain, disappointments, hurt, fear, and rejection to live her God-inspired life—embodying her true identity to live a life of truth and power!

In her spare time, she enjoys singing and reading, and she loves writing stories, books, poetry, declarations, and lyrics for inspirational songs. She is a wife to an awesome man of God and a mom to an amazing son and two fur babies whom she adores dearly and shares a home within Pearland, Texas.

Stay connected with Tonya:
Website: www.urrenewedmindmentor.com
Facebook Business Page:
"https://www.facebook.com/urrenewedmindmentor/"
Instagram:
https://www.instagram.com/onlytonyajohnson/
Facebook: www.facebook.com/tonya.johnson.503/
Twitter: https://twitter.com/TonyaJo07875490

Overcoming Identity Crisis

By Myisha Johnson

There are so many things that I could write about; God knows I have had my share of trials and tribulations; I mean, who hasn't? I prayed, and I sought God's face because the last thing I want to be is out of the will of God. So here we are.

IDENTITY CRISIS

An identity crisis is defined as a period of uncertainty or confusion in a person's life. This crisis occurs when a person's sense of identity becomes insecure and unstable.

Have you ever been so lost, insecure, and unstable that each day it is a process to even get out of bed? You wake up lost, go to sleep lost, every day forcing yourself to get up. Putting on a mask to hide all the pain, all the trauma, and confusion, trying to be something you are not. Carrying the weight on your shoulders, trying to ACT strong while being a Wife, a friend, a daughter, a mother, and, let's face it, the list goes on and on. As a mother, it was very challenging, my children were looking for me to affirm them, re-ensure them, and love them, but I was stuck in an Identity Crisis. You see, I could not love my children correctly or even give my husband all of me because I was too busy comparing myself to others; I was trying to change my identity; I wanted to be something I was not. I thought maybe if I changed the way I laugh, what I wear, and even how I look, surely, they would love me. All I have to do is talk like this and wear my hair like that; surely, I will receive the love and affirmation I have been longing for my whole life. Each day I opened my eyes, seeking validation from folks who could not even see that I was wearing a mask each day. Battling depression, suicidal thoughts and fighting for my life from the time I opened my eyes until... well, lol, it just never really stopped. Inadequate voices taunting you, whispering, "You're not beautiful," "no one could love someone like you," "who are you," "if you do this, they might like you," and "if you say this, you might get invited." They taunted me so much that I started to believe each word being spoken. I became a people pleaser; I smiled, I grinned, I helped everyone that I thought needed me. I ran myself ragged, and I was used and mistreated. I thought they could tell me who I was; maybe they could see the things I could not see. I know what you are thinking .... Girl, you should have just prayed about it or just simply told someone that you were feeling this way, but being stuck in sinking sand is so hard because all you're thinking is how I can get MYSELF out of this. After all, that's what I was taught my whole life; if you were raised in a household like mine, I'm sure you heard, "Don't ask nobody for nothing.... Get it out the mud" lol. So, I carried it, and it was soooo heavy.

As I looked in the mirror disgusted with the image that was before me. Wishing, longing, and I compared each flaw to someone I perceived was far more worthy than me. I would ask myself a series of questions; God created me in his image. Are you sure? Why would God create someone like me? I'm not beautiful; I'm not them; let's face it, I don't even know my purpose in life; God loves me unconditionally... are you sure? I stared in that mirror as tears fell from my eyes. I wanted purpose and fulfillment, but I just did not know how, which frustrated me.

I lost myself. I had put my hope and trust in things that helped me suppress every feeling of abandonment, every feeling of rejection, and every surface of inadequacy. Yea, you guessed it, alcohol, weed, parties, men. As long as I was high and drunk, I was good, but in all actuality, I was in an Identity Crisis,

Lost, wandering, and searching for my purpose. Screaming to the father, "Who am I, why am I here." Picture me running in the woods with no end in sight, just running, lost, scared, and hopeless. I sought out validation from everyone but God; I expected people to pour into me; I wanted them to tell me who I was; I wanted them to tell me my purpose, but how could they? Truth be told, they were just as lost as I was. I received prayer after prayer, but I just could not believe that God would even want to be bothered with someone like me.

One day I was lying in bed, and I heard a soft voice say, "I love you," now, just a little back story about me. I was always that scared child, the one scared of their own shadow. Lol, yes, that's me. So, when I heard it, I became scared, like it is literally no one else in this house but me. I heard it again, so soft and gentle, "I love you." I sat up in the bed, cut the TV off, and just sat there to tune into what was happening. I waited and waited; at this moment, I just sat still to hear it again to pinpoint where it was coming from. Time went by, and I heard nothing, so I decided to lay back down; as soon as my head hit the pillow, I heard, "You're beautiful."

I began to weep because, at that moment, I knew that it was God. At that moment, I felt overwhelmed by his love, grace, and mercy. At that moment, I came to myself just like the prodigal son did in the book of Luke. Luke 15:17. And when I came to myself, he said, "how many hired servants of my fathers have bread enough to spare, and I perish with hunger." To me, that scripture meant God has everything that I need; I don't have to be lost, I don't have to feel unworthy, I don't have to feel rejected, I don't have to perish with hunger, my father has everything I need. All I had to do was come to myself. The enemy wants us to feel like no one loves us and that no one cares. He wants us to walk in the posture of shame and guilt; He wants us to believe that God will not forgive us, but I am a living witness that God is waiting for us with open arms; he gave us beauty for ashes.

At that moment, I started my process of overcoming my Identity Crisis, and I say process because this was not something that was going to happen overnight. I knew that this would be a little difficult. Still, I also knew that once I overcame this, I would defiantly be breaking generational cycles and curses (Deuteronomy 30:19, "This day I call the heavens and the earth as witnesses against you that I have set before you life and death, blessings and curses, NOW CHOOSE LIFE SO THAT YOU AND YOUR CHILDREN MAY LIVE"). I not only wanted to embark on this journey for myself, but I wanted to do this for my children and my children's children.

I know you may be thinking, identity isn't that important; overcoming Identity Crisis doesn't make you God tough, but I can assure you that it is an essential factor in this walk with Jesus Christ. I am currently in a book club at my church, and Dr. Caroline Leaf calls the book that we are reading "Cleaning up Your Mental Health." Dr. Caroline Leaf states, *"When your identity is threatened, this can be reflected in the brain as an imbalance or lack of coherence, which will impact your cognitive functioning. When someone is going through an identity crisis, we see this reflected in the brain as low cognitive activity in the frontal lobe and pockets of high beta energy across the temporal lobe. This means that the non-conscious mind is trying to dissipate the toxic energy to restore some sense of balance, which will make you feel pretty bad about yourself, and, most likely, you won't react well in a challenging situation. **An identity crisis cuts to the core of your being and value, which will influence what you think, say, and do.** It can, if left unmanaged, severely affect your overall wellbeing* *and should be addressed sooner rather than later."* So, you see, it is very, very detrimental that we know who we are.

After we read a few chapters, I prayed to God for steps on how to overcome this because if I didn't, I would remain stuck, bearing no fruit.

Step 1: REPENT

I repented for not being grateful for how God made me; He said in his word that I am fearfully and wonderfully made. Wonderful is his work; I am his work, so that means I am wonderful, right? He created me in his image; he molded and shaped every curve, the way I smile, my color, and when he was done, he said, "It is Good." Therefore, any voice that tells me that I am not good enough is inadequate. PERIOD.

Psalms 139:14
Genesis 1:27

Step 2: Pray and Fast

I wanted to have a deeper relationship. I wanted to hear God more clearly. I wanted to look more like my father. So, I spent time with him; instead of seeking man's validation, I sought after God's face. He became everything to me, my best friend, my creative director, my life coach. He is MY EVERYTHING.

Joel 2:12

Step 3: Dig deep into God's word.

The Bible is the blueprint. There is nothing that we go through today that is not in the bible (nothing new under the sun). Therefore, I studied and applied it. Moses battled greatly with Identity Crisis; he desperately wanted to be known as a Hebrew, but instead he was seen as an Egyptian. He was born into one family but raised in another. When God called Moses, he tried to tell God (the one who created him) why he was not good enough, why he was unworthy, and how he was inadequate. He was in an Identity Crisis. Nevertheless, God quickly reminded Moses.
Exodus 3:10-15

Step 4: Change your environment.

Your environment tends to affect you and the way that you think. If you have a smoking or drinking problem, it is probably not a good idea for you to hang around smokers and drinkers. I was battling an Identity crisis, so I chose to surround myself with women who knew who they were. They were able to affirm me GENUINELY. They were able to remind me of who God says I am. Their confidence and boldness began to rub off on me.
Hebrews 12:1-2

I repeated these four steps until I was able to overcome them because repetition creates long-term memory. The more times something is repeated, the better it is remembered. While writing this chapter, the enemy and I tried to talk me out of sharing my testimony. Those inadequate thoughts started to surface again; I quickly had to remind myself who I was and who's I was.

So today, I encourage you to be unapologetic about how God made you. Fearfully and wonderfully made, above and not beneath, the head and not the tail, a chosen royal priesthood, a holy nation, and most importantly, God's special possession. My name is Myisha; I am BUILT GOD TOUGH, and I am UNAPOLOGETICALLY *ME.*

Be unapologetically you.

MYISHA JOHNSON

M
yisha is a Maryland native, a wife, a working mom, and an entrepreneur. She oversees a thriving company called The Lemonade Kidz. That has continued to grow since its conception. The

Lemonade Kidz is a business she created with her two youngest children. They wanted to start a business of their own, and Myisha being the super mom that she is, was eager to help and encourage her young entrepreneurs in the making. Myisha also serves as a valued worker in her community. She is participating in programs like Moving Dorchester Forward, which focuses on community engagement. She also heads a program called Confidence Breeds Success, where she volunteers her time and talents doing hair free for children in her community with the goal to build their confidence. Myisha also started a podcast called The Chit Chat, where she shares personal journeys and processes, she has experienced and endured during her spiritual walk with Jesus Christ. She is also very active in church (Living by Truth Ministry) as an usher and working in the youth department. Her faith has grown so much, and the revelation of God's love and his purpose for her life has brought her so much joy and peace. When Myisha is not out serving and working in her community, she enjoys reading, making music, spending time with family, and creating beautiful, long-lasting memories.

The War Within Me, My Life Off The Battlefield

By Keyonna Brinkley

Imagine being in the military for 15 years, retiring, and thinking that the battle is over, only to realize that the battle has just begun. For a great part of my childhood, I fought battles that were not my own which led me to make the ultimate decision to join the United States Army straight out of high school. To be exact, approximately less than 30 days from graduation, I was shipped off to basic training. I was scared but excited for this new way of life, the first time that I would be away from home and on my own, but I was up for the challenge.

Overall, military life was good; at least the first ten years were good. I was then given an assignment upon leaving Korea for an assignment that was about 2 hours from home (Delaware). I was so excited that I had traveled all over the world and now I would be closer to home. The unit that I was in was a very prestigious military unit, an infantry unit made up mostly of men besides the support staff. This assignment opened my eyes to so much, good and bad. In the military, to obtain authority and maintain certain positions, you attended boards such as promotion boards. These positions gave you more responsibilities as a Soldier, even putting you in charge of others. If you eventually became a commissioned/Non-Commissioned Officer, which I eventually did, which ultimately gave me more responsibility, including Soldiers that I was now in charge of supervising. There were also additional duties that we were tasked with, such as pulling overnight shifts (CQ) in the single soldiers' barracks for 24 hours.

The building we were in was an older house with dormitory rooms on two floors, upstairs and on the floor, that we pulled duty on. The basement was where the company staff had offices in the building, and that is where they conducted their daily duties. On duty, every hour, as the NCO in charge for the night, I had to walk back and forth to ensure that doors were closed and secure and that the Soldiers in the building were conducting themselves accordingly. One night, I made my checks on the upstairs floor and the floor where I was staffed at. Once I thought that the staff downstairs was out of the building, I went down to ensure that the offices in the basement were secure for the evening. It was at that time that I was approached by the person in charge of the arms room.

Earlier that day, he had called my office to ask me if I would be able to turn in my Nuclear Biological Chemical (NBC) mask today. I informed him that I had duty and would turn it in once I came for duty, but I had forgotten. I then let him know that the mask was upstairs at the CQ desk and that I would bring it back downstairs to him. I went upstairs to get the mask and returned to his office. I went into his office to turn in the mask, and this is where it went left. As I turned in the mask and began to head out, he followed me and proceeded to put his hand up against the door to try and keep me in his office. At that point, I didn't think much of it and went to grab for the door; at this time, he pushed me away from the door and began groping me while proceeding to turn off the lights.

I managed to push him away from me, kick him in his private, and walk out of the door, stating that "I'm not sure what kind of party you think this is, but this is not it."

I ran back to my CQ desk and called one of my friends that I worked with in the office and asked her to come down to the building when she got off. It was at this time that I explained to her what had happened, but I made it clear to her that I didn't want her to tell anyone because I was unsure at the time if I wanted to report it.

All night, I sat in that office contemplating my next move. At that point, I felt I was subordinate to him; who would believe me? The next day I was off because of the 24-hour duty, but upon returning to work, I had made up my mind that I wanted to let someone know what had happened. I called my supervisor and told him that I needed to speak with him about something that had happened while I was on duty. I explained the situation to him, and at that time, an investigation was started.

An investigation started, and it was at that time that my life in the military took a turn for the worst. It was also at that time that I found out that there were three other ladies in my unit that had also been victimized by this perpetrator. I felt embarrassed and scared, and so much ran through my mind at this time. During this process, I had people turn on me that were actually supposed to have my best interest, but it just seemed as if the higher-ups wanted to stick together instead of fighting for what was right.

People stopped talking to me; people started acting funny towards me, as if I was in the wrong. How could this be? I was not the only woman assaulted, which I thought would give me more grounds to deal with this guy and those that I trusted to be there for me at one of the worst points of my life. The whole process was torture. Tortured to the point where I and two other females had to go to court and were set to testify against this perpetrator. Luckily in court, the judge decided that he didn't want to put us through the testimony portion, which was such a relief. However, the military sentence given to this guy was humiliating, especially once it was exposed that he was discharged from another branch of service for the same misconduct. How could this be happening to me?

I felt like I was now part of an organization that was failing me on an opportunity and path that I chose, to get away, travel and defend my country and an organization such as the military allowed this to happen to me and so many other females and manage to humiliate them in the process. This process was painful, so painful that I couldn't even verbalize to my lover and confidant what happened to me and how I felt; I had to write a letter to him; it was just that sickening and painful. Painful to the point that I knew if I didn't fix how I was feeling, I was bound to lose my man; I knew then that I couldn't handle this battle on my own.

Things were happening to me that I was not understanding. I got to a point where I didn't want to be touched sexually, sex was becoming a turn-off, but I wanted kids, kids with my husband, and I also realized that he had needs too. I felt like that was it, I had to talk to someone, or that would be it for me and my future as a wife and mother. I had no idea where to start; counseling was seen as weak; in my raising, you handled situations on your own, "You didn't put people in your business!" THIS WAS NOW OUR BUSINESS, and it was affecting me heavily. It was at this time that I agreed to therapy to work on the issues that I dealt with daily. And to be able to focus on the things that I felt every woman wanted at one point in their life. I felt like this was my chance. Therapy brought out many traumas in my life, but the trauma that sat with me the most was that sexual trauma. The event in which I felt as though if I just told the truth, it would all be over; however, it haunted me daily. I was now in a situation in which I did all the right things, and it was now affecting me the most.

Therapy eventually put me back on the right track. I was able to use coping skills against the obstacles that I was facing, which put me in a much better place. Still not completely comfortable, but it was time for me to start the journey that I had prayed so hard for; to become a mother. Being faced with sexual trauma was a whole new introduction to this topic; there were still obstacles ahead of me that I knew that I had to fight to be able to continue along. It was during this time that I began transitioning out of the military, a different stressor of life. That transition was bittersweet for me; I felt like I had gained so much, but in a sense, I had lost a sense of myself, and I did not like that for me. Life had to get better.

During my transition from the military, I underwent intense therapy. It was during this time that I linked up with the best therapist that I know was sent my way by God. This woman allowed me to have a voice in front of others, allowed me to verbalize how I felt, and not once made me feel as if any of my trauma was my fault; she believed in me and all that I wanted for myself. It was then that I realized just how stuck I was in my head. I eventually received a medical discharge from the military and began a new way of life. With continuous therapy, my relationship began to blossom again, and I knew then that I was on the right track. It was at this time that I decided that with everything going on with me mentally and emotionally, I was ready to explore my options of becoming a mother as time was not on my side; I was 33.

My husband and I explored several options, and with different testing, we decided that, for several reasons, IVF would be the best route for us to take. At this point, I felt like I was ready for whatever was thrown my way. I had no idea what I was getting myself into, but I did know that this may be my only chance to give my husband his first biological child and my chance at becoming a mother.

So many emotions were overtaking me, but I knew I was willing to do whatever it took to make this happen for us. Extensive testing, followed by procedures and treatments, were all a part of the process. It was now time for our IVF cycle; we were ready and up for the challenge. The day came for our first transfer, and my nerves were all over the place, but I was ready, about as ready as I had ever been. Now came the time for the egg retrieval and to start hormone injections; this was way more than I had expected, but I was determined to push through. At the end of the cycle, there is a ten-day waiting period to test for pregnancy, the longest ten days of your life. Three weeks later, cycle one and ten days later, we find out that we are not pregnant.

I was devastated but determined not to quit, so we pushed forward with another cycle. Months later, I decided to jump back in and give it another try. This process was not as intense, but there was still a great deal of stress during this process, not to mention my husband was not able to be with me for most of my appointments, which happened during the early morning hours. I had to drive two hours there and back to these appointments at least three times a week, needing to be at those appointments by 5-6 AM. Luckily, I had an amazing support system that was able to step in when I needed them some days during this commute!

Three weeks passed, and this cycle is complete, only to receive another disappointment. At this point, depression set in heavy. I began to feel as if I was being punished for telling my truth all over again. Emotionally, I couldn't continue to endure this same pain and keep coming up with the same results. My husband and I then decided to take some time and revamp the process again when we were ready. He knew what this was doing to me physically and mentally and made it clear for me to take as much time as I needed. About a year goes by, and I decide I am ready to try this one last time.

This was it, I had one viable embryo left, and I knew that at this age, I did not think I would be able to complete a new cycle all over again if this was not a successful transfer. I remember my husband specifically asking me, "Are you emotionally ready to go through this again?" And I love and respect him for that. Because honestly, it made me think I wasn't sure if I was ready, but I began to think about everything that got us to this point and how much we had accomplished with just us; I wanted nothing more than to bring a child along this journey of love and life with us. I knew then, at that point; I was more than ready. Going into this cycle, my emotions were everywhere. Our first cycle failed after transferring one embryo, the second cycle failed with two transfers, and our last embryo was about to be transferred...I was sick.

We went forward with the transfer, and three weeks later, we finally heard the news we had waited so long for; we were pregnant. Talk about a miracle; with all that I had been through and endured, I never thought this day would come. God chose to bless us with our miracle baby in March 2017. If I never have another child in this lifetime, my heart is full because, through it all, God found it fit to bless us to be parents. I wouldn't change one bit of this process because God allowed my husband and I to enjoy and love each other in the midst of my storms. I am grateful that I have a man that loves me as he does and makes it clear that we can get through anything together. I realize now that things happen in our lives in God's timing and not ours, even with a mustard seed of faith. For those struggling, as hard as it may be, TRUST THE PROCESS! I realized that I was given these mountains to show others that they can be moved...in all situations, HAVE FAITH, FAITH OVER FEAR, AND KNOW THAT GOD'S GOT IT!

Remember that wars may end, but sometimes even his best Soldiers ALWAYS live with war wounds!

KEYONNA BRINKLEY

Keyonna Brinkley is a Retired Army Veteran and a first-generation college graduate. Keyonna graduated in the Behavioral Science field with her bachelor's degree, graduating with academic honors, and was inducted into Delta Epsilon Rho Honor Society. Shortly afterward, she received her Master's in

Applied Family Science with a 3.87 GPA. Keyonna joined the military less than a month after graduating from high school. Upon being medically discharged from the military after 15 years of active service, she decided to relocate back home with her husband in hopes of starting a family.

Upon returning home, Keyonna secured a position working in a Juvenile Detention Center that made her realize that her passion was to work with at-risk youth or at least be able to advocate for those who felt they could not advocate for themselves. During this time, she pursued her Bachelor's degree in Behavioral Health and later a Master's degree in Applied family science during the wonderful year of COVID while also being a stay-at-home mother/wife. Currently, Keyonna holds a position working for a Domestic Violence Program in her local community. Keyonna hopes to empower women with the many struggles women face that often go silent. I hope to be that VOICE of empowerment for those that feel stuck or as if they are alone.

Got Faith

By Lakesha Ballard

Mark 11: 22-26

I have always thought I was a woman with a great deal of faith; however, 2020 was the year that my faith was greatly tested. I remember going to the watch night service on December 31, 2019, and hearing the pastor preaching about all of those great things about the new year; I was in total agreement since 2019 was a rough year. I was ready for a new beginning I was prepared for new open doors and new opportunities. 2020 was going to be a pivotal moment for me and my triplets. They were graduating from high school. I was a proud mother.

Never did we imagine that in the next couple of months, the world would be in what I called a "be still" moment due to the COVID-19 pandemic. For the first time, everything changed. Schools closed; restaurants closed many churches closed their doors. Many people lost their jobs and or lost loved ones due to COVID 19 people started to lose faith in GOD. Many people had lost hope because they didn't know what tomorrow would hold for them or their loved ones. Students would not walk back into the schools that year and my triplet's hopes and dreams for their last year in high school were gone. No true graduation, no prom, no party or trip; it was gone just like that.

I remember going to a church that stayed open during the pandemic, and I went up for prayer, and the pastor said, "THE LORD WANTS YOUR YES... HE HAS NEED OF YOU."

I went home thinking about that and what that meant because I thought I gave him my yes, but when I think back it was a half-hearted yes... So, I prayed to GOD and gave him my YES. That's when my faith was put to the test. That next month I got COVID 19 and got fired from my JOB; my relationships with the ones I loved the most were tested. The devil was big mad about me giving GOD my YES. I know that now but at that time, I didn't know what was going on, but I know I couldn't give up on GOD. GOD is so good and will give us what we need when we need it. I remember sitting in my living room with my now husband, watching church online because I was still in quarantine. While praying I got the gift of the Holy Spirit with evidence of speaking in tongues. GOD knew that I would need the comforter like never before in the next couple of months.

During this time, I noticed that my middle daughter was more negative and nastier and just hateful. She would pick a fight with her sisters. She didn't care who it was. She was just nasty. I would always think, how could she be so negative? I would speak positively to her, and not just to her but to all my children, as I'm a mother of four. I remember telling her that I loved her, and she wouldn't believe that I loved her, not just me but anyone. She didn't even believe she was my child; remember, she is a triplet. I always enjoyed spending time with my children; however, every time we did something, it would always end in some type of disagreement. I was already going through my own "storm," so I started to distance myself from my own girls.

It was during this time that I got closer to GOD like never before, even with my health scare, no income, and my relationship with the ones I loved the most were all tested. At that time, I realized many times in my life, I would put my trust in man and not fully in GOD. During this time, I had to trust GOD for everything, not just the small things but for the big things. The supernatural things. There were many times I didn't understand why I had to go through what I was going through, even down to why I couldn't get my unemployment like everyone else.

I remember Holy Spirit speaking to me, saying that if my unemployment were released when I wanted it to, then I would not learn to trust him for everything.

I think it was around October that I noticed that the devil tried everything to get me to turn my back on GOD and not trust him, but everything I was going through pushed me closer to him. So, the enemy came for blood with the ones I loved the most. My daughter, what I thought was just a nasty attitude, was depression and suicidal thoughts, and she was cutting on herself, and what made it even worse was she questioned if GOD was real and said she was going to Hell.

I began praying and fasting for my loved ones, and I remember GOD saying that "HE" GOD would heal, deliver and restore. So, what do you think happened next? One might think things got better, no ma'am, no sir, things got worse. I thought it was something I was doing that was making them worse. I know that was nothing but the trick of the enemy wanting me to give up on GOD. All this was new to me. Yes, I knew GOD and how good he is, but this time it was different. Once I gave GOD my YES, my real Yes, he was making me into a prayer warrior. I had to stop trying to fight in the natural and fight in the supernatural and not with my own power but with the power of the Holy Spirit. Ephesian 6:12 KJV, "For we wrestle not against flesh and blood, but against principalities against powers, against the rulers of the darkness of this world, against spiritual wickedness in high places."

Thanksgiving dinner that year was a little different due to the pandemic; it was just my mom, my kids, and myself. That's when I found out things with my daughter were worse than ever; she went from being negative to depressed to thoughts of suicide to cutting on herself. At dinner, she didn't eat, and she loved Baked Mac and Cheese; she would say it made her sick and she didn't need to eat because she wanted to die. I remember sitting in the living room talking to her and looking at her left arm. She had cut herself all up her arm and my oldest. My heart dropped. It was tough to see and hear that.

I told her that if she continued, I would have her sent to the hospital for a mental health evaluation, but she was 18 years old. I couldn't force her, but I was prepared to get the law involved. That night I went home and prayed and cried out to GOD; GOD spoke so plainly and told me that he had her in the palm of his hand. I wish I could say that at that point, everything got better, but that's not what happened. It got even worse.

Two days later, my oldest daughter called me and said my daughter was cutting herself and she had written a suicide note. I called 911. When the police arrived, she continued telling them she didn't want to live anymore, so she went to the hospital to be evaluated for mental health. The hospital determined she needed in-patient treatment. I was heartbroken and didn't understand, but I had to trust GOD and his plan as he told me he had her in the palm of his hand. She stayed in the mental hospital for about a week. They started her medication for her depression, but she would only take that for about a month. She was also supposed to see a therapist. She went back three times at best. Nothing changed with my daughter. I might even say, she got worse. She was still dealing with the spirit of depression and suicide, and the enemy was using her to come after me to hurt me with her words like it was my fault because she was like that, that I had never been there for her or her siblings. My daughter had to return to the mental hospital in three months for the same thing. I would pray and ask God to wrap his loving arms around her and let her know he was real.

As I continued to get closer to GOD, GOD would wake me up between the hours of 2 am and 3 am, and he prepared me for things to come; so many times, in my life, I would pray to GOD and ask for things of this world, but now I needed to trust GOD for the supernatural. In January 2021, as I was praying, God said it was a matter of my heart. GOD highlighted Mark 11:22-26. I had faith in GOD, but I still was hurt by the things that my daughter said, but I needed to forgive because I wanted to be forgiven, but more importantly, I didn't want anything to block my prayers for the people that I was praying for, especially my daughter.

One day I was on my way to work at 6:30 am. GOD spoke to me and told me to hug His daughter, so I replied, "OK, GOD, when I get off tonight, I'll go and hug her." I worked 12 hours, and my drive home was 30 mins; I had forgotten but thank God for the Holy Spirit that will bring all things back. I'm not going to lie, I was tired and didn't want to go, but I did. I walked in the door and went to her room. I told her to get up for me to hug her, I held her for a couple of minutes, told her I loved her and would talk to her later, and walked out the door.

A couple of weeks later, I was going to take a road trip to a church down south, about an eight-hour drive, and I asked my girls if they wanted to go. My middle one said yes; I was more than happy because she has always said no to everything and especially church. I thought if I could get her to that pastor, she would see the spirit that my daughter was dealing with and cast that spirit out her. That was not GOD's plan. I laugh at it now, but that pastor was away that Sunday, but there I was, trying to do GOD's work, and he didn't need any help; I just needed to trust him.

When we got home, I prayed with my daughter with some other friends, and she said I don't "feel what I feel" (Holy Spirit). She shared that day I came over "out of the blue" to hug her. She was going to commit suicide that day. With tears in my eyes, I looked at my daughter and told her I had no idea of knowing that, but GOD did and how much he loved her. In that next breath, she said I still don't want to live. She (that Spirit) started laughing at me. I looked into my daughter's eyes and said, " Luke 10: 19 Behold, I give unto you the power to tread on serpents and scorpions, and over all the power of the enemy and nothing shall by any means hurt (me or my daughter) I knew that I was talking to that Spirit because that smile turned to a look like oh she not playing with me anymore.

Ever since that day, for about two years, my daughter's outlook on life has changed. GOD delivered her from those spirits that were controlling her. I just had to have faith and trust God that he would do what he said. I remember one day I cried out to GOD saying I wanted to give up and throw in the towel, and GOD said "NO!!" And to trust him. When I look back at 2020, I'm grateful to GOD because what I thought might have broken me GOD was there, and he was building me to be the women of GOD he needed me to be; that I do not need to look to man because he shall supply everything I/WE NEED. WE JUST NEED TO HAVE FAITH.

MARK 11: 22-26

And Jesus answering saith unto them, Have faith in God. For verily I say unto you, That whosoever shall say unto this mountain, Be thou removed, and be thou cast into the sea; and shall not doubt in his heart, but shall believe that those things which he saith shall come to pass; he shall have whatsoever he saith. Therefore I say unto you, What things soever ye desire, when ye pray, believe that ye receive them, and ye shall have them. And when ye stand praying, forgive, if ye have ought against any: that your Father also which is in heaven may forgive you your trespasses. But if ye do not forgive, neither will your Father which is in heaven forgive your trespasses.

LAKESHA BRASBY

My name is **Lakesha Brasby**. I am a wife, mother and daughter. I have worked in healthcare for over 25 years with the last 12 years working as a nurse in nursing homes, correction, addiction and Labor and Delivery. I am a servant of the God; I just want to be used by Him; I love helping GOD's people.

NOT AGAIN...

BY CAPRI LEE

Have you ever felt happy and excited but also angry and confused? Well, I have. My mental state was discombobulated, and I didn't know how to feel or what the future held. I immediately began to think, "How could I end up pregnant during my last year of high school? - I am not built for this."

Everything seemed to be going right for me. I had just returned from visiting colleges with the assistant principal, and life was falling into place. I wanted to be what everyone expected "Capri" to be. Being pregnant would mean that the naysayers were right. I was disappointed in myself for becoming a statistic, and I could not handle it, emotionally or mentally.

January of 2001 (I do not remember the exact day), but I can recall I just felt meh. Throughout that day, I gradually became nauseated. My first thought was that it was the "time of the month." But then again, this felt different. My first intention was to go to the nurse's office and lay down. Instead, I decided to walk to the Sex-ed room.

The Sex-ed room was a place to get contraceptives and set clinic appointments, but often students went to hang out. The teacher in there was the coolest, but this day, I didn't want anyone to see me walking in there, so I was as discrete as possible. The Sex-ed Lady and I previously established a rapport, so I was comfortable talking to her about anything. With my head hanging low and tears lingering in my eyes, I entered her room. She greeted me with the same excitement as she normally did. Simultaneously, my friend Nish walked in, noticed my sadness, and asked, "What's wrong?"

The tears left my eyes and rolled down my cheeks. I felt the little bit of strength I had leave my body. Then I said, "I think I'm pregnant."

They both exclaimed their disbelief and disappointment. At this point, we all saw my pregnancy as a hindrance. The Sex-ed Lady gave me a pregnancy test, and I proceeded to do what was needed. After taking the pregnancy test, I placed it on the sink and returned to the Sex-ed room. Nish and the Sex-ed Lady went into the bathroom, awaiting the results. As I sat there alone, stinking thinking abruptly entered my psyche. The ugly face of low self-worth took over my thoughts. I thought of all the people that would be disappointed. Every question that could be asked, I thought of. Am I going to keep it? Will I be a good mother? Would I still graduate? Can I still cheer? Every question remained unanswered until I knew for sure what my fate was.

I heard footsteps getting closer and closer. My heart was beating faster and faster. For a split second, I believed that I was not with child. They walked in. Both faces were overflowing with tears. I knew. Seventeen and pregnant was my story. But how? And why? Why would God allow this to happen when I have so much going for me? This can't be my life – But it was.

May 31, 2001, I graduated with a cosmetology license and the biggest belly in the class! Yes, I was with child and was due to have my baby boy in August. Life was happening and fast. My son's father and I began receiving gifts for our new baby boy as well as gifts for our new residence. Arriving a month earlier than the expected due date, on July 20, 2001, my son De'Mere was born. This was one of the happiest days of my life, but the happiness was short-lived. Directly after I gave birth, well, I was able to love on him for a few seconds, Mere was taken from my arms, and the medical staff prepared him for transport. I wasn't even able to give him a name.

He was identified as "Baby Boy Lee." He was born with a few difficulties: He was unable to maintain his body temperature, he had jaundice, and there were issues with his coordination. Mere would stop breathing when he sucked on the bottle, and all of these things landed him at The Johns Hopkins Hospital for five days. While my son was on his way to Baltimore, Easton Hospital suggested that I stay another night because of the excretion of meconium, or the baby's first poo, was in my system. Being forced to separate from my first love was impossible, and I couldn't cope. It felt as if my beating heart was snatched through my chest cavity and flaunted in my face. I could not find it within myself to remain positive, but what I did know was that God would never bring me that far to leave me. The support system Mere's father and I had was beyond awesome, making it easier to become accustomed to parenthood. It also helped us to make sense of what we were going through. I adjusted to being selfless and providing for another human being. After all of the negative feelings and thoughts, I embraced what was gifted to me by God, MOTHERHOOD. I realized that he trusted me to train up this child.

Fast forward to about September of 2005, Mere was doing well and preparing to attend Head Start. Being a mother had its uncertain moments, but I did what I had to do with all I had. Mere's father and I had our ups and downs, and the love began to fizzle away. Amid our "not-so-good times," I was reintroduced to one of Nish's cousins, whom I knew of but not on a personal level. We spent a lot of time together and one thing led to another.

Around the beginning of November, I began feeling queasy while walking Mere to the bus stop. I really didn't think much of it. I continued with my daily routine. Nish and I often walked from the bus stop together as she had two boys of her own. We began to have a normal conversation. I slid in the fact that I was not feeling the best, and she gave me that look like, "Girrrrl!"

Instantly, I began thinking, "Not Again." There was no way on God's green earth that I could be pregnant again, especially not after one sexual encounter. Those were the thoughts of my immature mind. Nish's cousin was at her house at the time. She ran up the steps excited and laughing. I did not find it funny. How can this happen again? I'm not ready for a second child. I don't know if I can financially support another baby. Will he help? What will my mom say? What will I tell Mere's dad? The thought of having two children by two different men made me sick to my stomach. I did not want that for me. Nonetheless, he was ecstatic. I wasn't. He told me I would have a son. I really did not care what it would be because I did not want it. I went to the clinic to get a pregnancy test. And yes, again. Reality punched me in the face, and it hurt. My only mission was to abort this unwanted baby. I expressed my feelings to him, and we ultimately agreed that it would be my final decision. I made an appointment at the abortion clinic for that next week.

The day was here. It was time to get rid of this baby so I could get on with my regular life. I checked in and sat down in the waiting area. An hour went past. I went to the receptionist's window to see if they had forgotten about me. She explained that the doctor had an emergency and would not be able to maintain his appointments. This can't be life. It was life, and I rescheduled. The next appointment came, and I was punctual. I got checked in, and as I was about to slide my debit card, the receptionist informed me that the system was down. Here we go again, but this time there is a solution! I told her I'd just run to the ATM really quick and be right back. I did just that, but to my surprise, the ATM was down. Not again. My heart starts beating fast. I became extremely anxious. I thought I had everything figured out, but God had another plan. I called Nish's cousin and explained why I could not go through with it.

Over the course of a few weeks, I became more comfortable with my situation. Just as I settled in to become a mother of two, a phone call disrupted my way of life again. I answered the phone and heard, "You have a collect call from, Dip" on the other end.

It was my unborn child's father. I could not believe what I was hearing. Once connected to him, he asked if I had seen the news. Although I was puzzled, I responded, "Yes."

He explained that the news story was about him and he was facing a life sentence for first-degree murder. The biggest lump formed in my throat. My heart fell to my feet. My child's father was about to go away forever. No, not again. How could I end up in this situation?

I didn't know how I was going to deal with this while being pregnant, but I did. Dip called regularly to check on his unborn child. On May 13, 2006, I was on my way out to dinner. It was happening; I was about to give birth. I went to Easton Hospital for the second time. I was told that my amniotic sac was leaking. The doctor examined me and suggested I stay overnight so they could keep a close eye on me. Due to the leakage, I had to be induced. It was weird not to have the father of my child with me during labor, but Mere's father was supportive. I also had my Godmother Evon and my friends, Rufonda and Tonya. Right before I went into labor, I called the facility where Dip was incarcerated to see if he could at least be on the phone while his child was being born. They agreed, but the warden had to verify that I was truthful, and the collect call had to be received through the hospital's phone. He called back right away and was able to hear his son, Da'Jour, enter the world screaming on Mother's Day, May 14, 2006.

Life got real for me. But I reminded myself that God navigated me through the last pregnancy and delivery, so why would he leave or forsake me now? I was reminded that God's word is a lamp unto my feet and a light unto my path (Psalms 119:105). It may have seemed a little dark then, but I knew joy came in the morning. I felt shameful and felt as if the whole town was talking about me. I'm sure they were, but I was reminded that greater is He in me than in the world (1 John 4:4). I knew that God was faithful and that He would provide. I realized that I had to go through this to be a voice for others. He placed me in an educational setting where I would come in contact with those who deal with situations, I have knowledge in. God was using me and preparing me for a time like this.

I realized that no weapon formed against me, or my sons would prosper (Isaiah 54:17). I speak life into them daily. Especially Da'Jour. It has not been easy for him growing up with an incarcerated father. He turned

17 on May 14, 2023; ironically, his birthday was Mother's Day again. His birthday will serve as a reminder of how God helped me over. Jour's father has served 16 years so far and is still incarcerated. He copes well, and they have an amazing relationship. I am grateful for everyone who has been a part of my support system. Despite getting myself into these situations, I knew God would bring me out. I now understand and comprehend that if not ME, then who. I was built for this. Neither situation then nor can a situation now break me. Why? Because I am built GOD TOUGH.

CAPRI LEE

Capri **Lee** is a devoted mother of two sons, a committed educator, and a social justice advocate. Capri is also the co-founder of the comedic duo, *"Cousins Cuttin' Up"*, who opened for headliner, *Real Talk Kim* at Festa Della Donna (2019). She was also featured in [*King of Kings*], a major stage production with gospel greats, Shirley Caesar and James Fortune. Capri is also integral to students' success as a middle school educator. In 2022, she became an International Best-Selling Author, as she was featured in the "I Am Stronger Than the Storm" anthology. Although Capri is small in stature, her voice is substantial when it comes to matters of equality and justice, with her being a major proponent of the Maryland State Legislatures, *Anton's Law*, a law that provides more transparency for families impacted by the conduct of law enforcement officers. Capri believes that laughter is the gateway to positivity and relays that message to anyone she encounters.

Capri Lee
mogulcapri01@gmail.com
Facebook and Instagram: Capri Pritty Lee

Just Existing

By Monique Dames

Suffering the loss of a sibling is something I thought I would never experience in my lifetime. Naturally, being the oldest child of both of my parents, you think that you should die first. But of course, we all know that we do not know God's plans. On May 28, 2021, one of my sisters passed away unexpectedly. When I got that call, my reaction was, What? Dead? It did not register with me. My mind went blank; I could not form any other words; I was in total and utter shock. It felt like someone had hit me in my chest. I was so lost. What was I supposed to do next? At this point, I was numb.

How did I just lose the person that held all my secrets? I literally could and would say anything to her and not feel like I would be judged. Believe me; I told her some crazy things. She would just listen, sometimes laugh as only she could, and then provide sound guidance if I requested it, who am I kidding, even when I did not request it. She was my phone riding partner. She would say that I was always on the road, and I was and still is. When I was on the last leg of a road trip, she would talk to me until I was home then she would say, "You gonna quit using me."

My sister and I have the same father and did not grow up together. In fact, I did not meet her until 2005. At that point, I was 24, and she was 23. I live in Maryland, and she lived in Florida. That did not matter because our bond was unbreakable.

This was a really hard time in my life. I guess I really did not know how to grieve. I am always busy doing one thing or the other, so I kept busy. I cried, of course, but when I did, I would try to cry when I was alone. If I was out in public and felt the need to cry, I would go off to myself. I preferred to grieve alone. I did not want to answer the "Are you ok?" question; I did not really know how to respond to that, but I really was not ok. For the next few months, I just existed. I went to work, I went to the gym, I went to church, I saw my trainer, I went to cheer practice, I was visited by friends, I went to my home on the eastern shore (Maryland), and I spent time with my family. People constantly checked on me, but I still felt all alone. I was literally sinking and did not realize it. I felt like I had no one—the one person I wanted to talk to, I couldn't. I felt like I had to function normally because I was supposed to be strong for everyone else. So, I continued to exist.

You know, taking time to grieve is very important, but I could not. I wanted to keep busy because...what happens when I stop? I had to move along with life and be there for others. In the meantime, I was slowly losing my mind. I tried to keep it together all the time. Listen, I know better than to question God, but I couldn't help but wonder why this happened, how did this happen? So many unanswered questions. Conversations that would never happen. I literally was praying to keep it together and crying out to God; please help me! My heart is broken! I couldn't believe I slipped into depression. People that are supposed to be strong are supposed to just keep going. How could this happen to me? I literally was existing every day— no real intentions. However, I knew that I could not go on that way.

Prior to my sister's passing, I started working out regularly. I would get up in the morning before work to work out. I would get up at 4:30 am to get to my gym by 5 am when the doors opened. I would go that early because there weren't many people there at that time. I started to find that this was the best time of day to talk with God for me. I had more clarity at that time and was able to focus. It became my favorite part of the day, and it still is. On the days I went to the gym in the morning, I was more upbeat, I did not have as many mood swings, and I could get through the day. Sometimes when I'm in the gym, I find myself just worshiping God. I listen to songs that minister to my spirit as I attempt to get through my workout. Sometimes I sing out loud and dance, especially when I am in the classroom. I am usually there by myself.

Working out quickly became the outlet I used to grieve. However, as I think about it, it was not the working out part that got me through. It was that I was spending that time with God. My mind is so clear during that time. I felt things starting to shift. I no longer cried alone. I was now laughing, remembering the things she would say. I was able to remember the good times with her. My sister's laughter was infectious. You couldn't help but laugh when she did. I remember the last time I talked to her; she had me laughing so hard. Casting my cares on God, I was starting to see my way out of depression. Things got so bad for me mentally at one point. I made a snap decision, and I quit my job for one with less responsibility, or so I thought. Thankfully, I heard God say go back, and I did just that very quickly.

I literally felt like I was not going to make it through this storm. God continues to heal me through this journey. I am still a work in progress, and I have my moments. But I know with God, anything is possible. People will not always understand what you are going through. I have learned that you cannot put your faith in people because they are human, and they may fail you. However, you can always put your faith in God. He will not fail. I am so thankful that I was able to come out on the other side of this with my right mind. I have a testimony that God is a healer. When you cannot see any other way, He is there. All you have to do is trust Him. He continues to guide me daily. There are times when I will try to do things my own way, but I get nowhere. I am so glad that I learned to allow God to direct me. The thought that I will leave is that when you are going through different trials in your life, you do not have to just exist. All you have to do is trust that God has a plan for you, and He does not fail!

Monique "Coach Mo" Dames

Monique was born and raised on the Eastern Shore, Maryland. She has an MBA with a concentration in Human Resources from Strayer University and BS in Business Management from Delaware State University. Monique and her daughter relocated to Baltimore, so Monique could continue to pursue her career in Human Resources. She has worked in Human Resources for the last 13 years. Currently, she is a Classification and Compensation Manager.

Monique also coaches All-Star Competitive Cheer with My G.I.R.L.S. All Stars, Inc in Baltimore City, where she enjoys teaching athletes the fundamentals of cheer. Her passion is training young ladies to build their endurance, increase their strength and practice healthier habits. Recently, she decided to continue building upon her passion and pursuing certifications in personal training and nutrition coaching. She recently started a health and wellness business, Mo Energy Fitness, where she plans to offer personal training services to young ladies and women.

Contact Information:
Email: mdames03@gmail.com
IG: getfit_withmo_ or msdames03
Facebook: Monique Dames

Unmatched Strength
By Antoinette Redji

One hot summer day, as the fan blew warm air around, Antoinette walks into the room to see her twin sister Sarah lying across the bed. As she walks in, her twin sits up on the bed; Antoinette looks at her and says, "Sarah, you should let me do your hair."

Sarah responds, "No, Antoinette, because you not going to get me in trouble; you know mommy told us not to touch her black hair gel. You never listen, Antoinette. That's why your dumb butt always getting in trouble."

Antoinette tells her to shut up and that she won't get in any trouble if we only use a little bit; she won't even notice. "So come on, sit here, I'm going to do it, and it's going to look cute, too sis." Says Antoinette. Antoinette jumps down off the bed and walks into the bathroom and grabs her mom's black gel off the counter.

As she walks back into the room, Sarah says, "I don't know, Antoinette, I don't think this is a good idea. I think Mommy is going to notice."

Antoinette responds, "Chill girl, it's okay; stop being scared all your life. Do you want to be cute or not?"

Sarah says, "Yeah, I do, but I'm going to do yours too, and you better not lie on me if Mom finds out."

Antoinette responds, "Oh hush, sis, I'm not going to lie, plus it's okay because she's not going to find out."

"Umm hmmm," Sarah replies as she rolls her eye at her.

Annoyed but excited, Antoinette begins to do Sarah's hair slapping about three handfuls of gel on her hair and swooping it into a high ponytail.

"Okay, sis, all done," Antoinette exclaims. Her sister turns around, looks in the mirror, and says, "Ooh, I'm cute now, alright, Antoinette; now it's your turn."

Antoinette looks at her and says, "Oh, I changed my mind. I don't want my hair done now."

Sarah yells, "What?"

As she looks at Antoinette, irritated and angry because she lied to her. She dips her hand in the gel and slaps Antoinette with the gel. Both girls yelling and screaming at each other. Their mother, who was in the other room and comes rushing in where the girls were. As the room door flew open, their mother says, "What in the world is going on in here?" Before we got a chance to answer, her face turned fire-red.

In a calm voice, their mother said, "I know that isn't my black hair gel I told you not to touch?"

Suddenly, Antoinette's sister burst out crying, pointing her finger, saying, "I told Antoinette not to touch it."

Antoinette says to her sister, "But you let me do it, so we're both in trouble."

As Antoinette folds her arms. Their mother rushes out of the room and comes back in with a belt. She whipped both of the girls. The black gel was flying everywhere, all over the bed, walls, and ceiling! When she finished, both girls were crying. Their mom turns around as she walks out and yells, "Now clean it up!"

The funny thing is, my sister was right, and we definitely got into trouble. As the saying goes, if I knew then what I know now, I would have listened to my mama when she said some things were off-limits and not to be touched. Everything has its time and season, but you see, with me, I was in too much of a hurry, wanting to grow up and do my own thing without being told what to do, apart from anything or anyone. There was one person that could control me and be my voice of reason. That person was my father. I am and always will be a daddy's girl. My father is literally my heart in human form. When I was 11 years old, he went to prison for almost eight years. In his absence, I searched for him in every boy I came around.

Unfortunately, at the age of 12, I lost my virginity and became pregnant. Forced to leave middle school, because being 12 and pregnant in middle school was not the ideal look. I was so scared, humiliated, and embarrassed. I was a baby carrying a baby. Months pass, and now it was time for me to give birth. As I laid in the hospital bed, scared, timid, and exhausted, my room was full of family and friends. Ten centimeters dilated, and I'm ready to push as I'm fading in and out and in, pushing with all my might. I hear the nurse yell, "Hand me the forceps and the suction cup!"

At that moment, it seemed like the earth stood still. That was the longest five minutes of my life. Finally, the baby was out. So much excitement and happiness filled the room. Then suddenly, the nurse clears all my family out of the room, and a swarm of doctors and nurses rush in. I start to panic and really cry because I really don't know what's happening or what's even going on.

Tired and exhausted with the little breath I have left, I ask, "Is the baby, ok?" No one answered me. Instead, all the doctors and nurses took the baby into another room. Moments later, my doctor returned with a look of depression and horror on his face. He begins to explain to me that there was fluid and blood on the baby's brain, and the baby did not make it. I was so shocked and confused that I couldn't cry or even show any emotion. I was completely numb. As months and years went by, I replaced the absence of my dad with boys and wanting to replace the baby I had lost. So, when I was seventeen, I got pregnant again.

But this time, it was going to be different. I got pregnant on purpose. I wanted the baby I had lost also five years before. I wanted the baby, but my baby's father did not want me. He was young; he didn't want a committed relationship, let alone a baby. He cheated, lied, and made me cry more than I could remember. Once he cheated and I found out about it. He got angry with me and pushed my belly into the corner of a table. I was eight months pregnant at the time. I rushed to the door to leave, and my leg got caught, so he slams the door on my leg. I finally got free and walked five miles in the dark through a graveyard to get home. The next day he called me and apologized. He said he was so sorry, and it would never happen again. But that was nothing but a lie. Eventually, I decided to leave the relationship and take care of my baby on my own. I made do with the help of my family.

About three years later, I got pregnant again, but this time it wasn't on purpose. There was no way I could keep this baby. I wasn't even in a relationship with the baby's father. We were college friends. This was not supposed to happen. So, I decided I was going to terminate the pregnancy. As I pull up to the clinic, I was scared but so sure I was doing the right thing. There is no way I could take care of two babies on my own, and I'm not with either of their fathers. I walked into the clinic and signed in. As I take my seat, my nerves were going crazy. A nurse comes to the door and calls my name. I got up and followed her. She takes me into this cold room. And handed me a hospital dress.

"Take off all your clothes and get on the bed," said the nurse. Then she walks out of the room, and I do as I am told. Late, the doctor returns. He walks into the room and tells me to lay down. There is a monitor in front of him as he squirts this cold gel on my belly and tells me I am about three months pregnant. He then wipes my belly and tells me to open my legs.

At this point, I'm shaking like a leaf. Before he could say or do anything else. I jumped up off the bed, grab my clothes, and ran out of the office. I get in my car, and I'm screaming and crying, asking, "God, how can I do this? GOD, please help me! I can't! I can't kill my baby! GOD, PLEASE HELP ME, PLEASE!"

The spirit of God came into that car like no other. I felt safe, secure, and strengthened. I knew for sure that God was going take care of my babies and me and everything was going to be alright. It was true; God showed up and did exactly that.

About six months later, I met another guy whom I knew for sure was the one. He was going to be my husband and a father to my children. So, what did I do? UMM... I got pregnant again. When he found out I was pregnant, he turned on me. He started spreading lies that I was trying to trap him and that the baby I was carrying was not his child. I was devastated – AGAIN! How could this happen to me again? Pregnant by a man who doesn't want me. I'm not even 21 with three kids by three different men. No, this is not real. This can't be my life. Nine months passed, and I had my third living child. We got a paternity test, and he was the father.

My third child's father apologized and said he was sorry and that he wanted to be there for his child. So, we tried to make it work. But it didn't; he was unfaithful and unwilling to settle down and marry. So, before my third child was one year old, I was a single mother with three children by three different men and not with any of them. But in those moments when it was just me and my children, God showed up for me and them in ways I could never imagine. I was working a 100% commission job and have never lived off the government or welfare. God has always provided in a way I could never imagine. I have never lived in the image of the single black mother statistic of barely making it and living off the government to survive. I am made God tough, overcoming every obstacle and every challenge that has ever come my way because my God is a God that provides and fights for me.

ANTOINETTE REDJI

Antoinette Redji is prosperous. She brings prosperity to any environment, connection, or relationship she encounters. Antoinette is tenacious no matter what life throws her way; she keeps a firm grip on who she is and what she believes. Antoinette is inquisitive concerning the kingdom of God; she desires to understand the deep mysteries of

God. She is also nonchalant and remains calm in certain instances as she rolls with the punches. Antoinette is always consistent in her personality; you will never have to guess what version of her is going to show up. She is always the same, with a smile and genuine love.

Antoinette is a co-partner of the Holy Chicks Droppin' Nuggets Podcast and a Co-Owner of the Runway Station boutique. Antoinette is also a wife and a mother of three beautiful children.

Antoinette Redji
Ahickma5@gmail.com

IG - @God_angel88

FB - @Antoinette Redji

Podcast - @HolyChicksDroppinNuggets

Your Pain Is Your Purpose:

By Alishia Potter

I was 26 years old with a baby on my hip and a baby in my belly when I started the painful and devastating journey through divorce. At the time, I was a high school teacher traveling an hour each way to work. Worried that I was about to become a single mom of two stair-step kids, I immediately returned to school to work on my Master's Degree. I figured that it would make more sense for me to have a job that didn't come home with me so that I could be present for my kids.

As I was trying to pick up the broken pieces of my life, they kept falling apart, and in the last semester of my Graduate school year, my children and I became homeless. We became homeless and had to move into a homeless shelter for women. I was shattered. I felt so embarrassed. I felt like I had failed as a mom. I was so full of bitterness and anger. Think of the blackest thing you've ever seen: a black patent leather shoe, an old crackled black leather jacket, a heap of dark unused charcoal. That's how dark I was with bitterness. I was angry with God; I was angry with the church, and I was angry with life.

From day one, I had never really been attracted to my then-husband. I saw all of the red flags and heard all of the sirens. Yet, I still allowed myself to fall prey to the internal and external pressure I felt. At the age of 23, I was insecure and had very low self-worth. I had been battling loneliness and depression and even a bout with anorexia. I had a very poor self-image. Those were my internal pressures. "Who else is gonna want me?" I asked myself, after having had so many failed relationships. He had been showing interest in me for years, according to the external pressures around me. Yet, the flags that I saw were so glaring, and just plain and simple, he wasn't my "type" (whatever that was at the time.)

I just kept rejecting the idea. The external pressures went from a schoolyard feel of, "Steve really likes you!" and "You two make a cute couple." To the *church lingo of,* "God's not gonna give you what you want; he's gonna give you what you need." To the implications of "being disobedient" if I didn't move forward with this undesired *yet* desired relationship.

So, I did it. In January of 1998, we got married. It was fast and furious, and we didn't make it to our first anniversary.

So, in the process of going through homelessness and living in the homeless shelter, I was going to church and wearing "the mask." I even put "masks" on my children in the sense that you couldn't tell from looking at us that we had just gotten clothes from the storage unit, brought them to the shelter, got dressed all nice and pretty for church, smiling on the outside but broken on the inside. I endured painful encounters, such as watching my then-husband, who was estranged from us, and a deacon and trustee at the church, walk by me and our children like he didn't even know who we were. He did that also while I was pregnant with our daughter.

Three years before becoming homeless, when I was pregnant with our daughter, I ended up being placed on complete bed rest by my OB/GYN due to pregnancy complications. I had a history since the first child of having what they termed "at risk" pregnancies. I couldn't really lift anything. I couldn't walk too long. Caleb was still in an infant car seat. In my faithfulness to be in church services, I would struggle to wobble myself out of the car to get inside the church carrying Caleb in his heavy car seat with no help as I watched their father rush down the aisle to busy himself with church things like he didn't know me - like he didn't know our son – like I was invisible.

While no one around us held him accountable for at least showing common decency and Christian love, it would be five years more that I would experience this in this small 100-member church before I would have the courage to leave such an unhealthy and toxic environment after a 15-year commitment to that ministry.

While living at the homeless shelter, I was completing my last semester of internships in Washington, DC, which was more than a 2-hour drive from where I lived. I would wake up and mop the shelter floors, as required, drop off my children at a home daycare by 6:00 am, and be on the road to get to my internship by 9:00. I had recently been laid off from my job once I was given an ultimatum to choose completion of my internship hours over my job and so many days, I didn't have the gas money. I was only receiving a $500.00 stipend for the whole semester, but God made a way.

As I approached the 29th day of living in the shelter, I recall the owner, whom I had only seen in passing once or twice, walked by me in the hallway that day, and he said, "Don't forget today is your last day."

I had recently been advocating for myself with the shelter's Social Worker for a lengthier stay because 30 days just wasn't enough time for someone to get her life together. Someone who was battling depression; someone who was battling hopelessness; someone who had barely any income and was working really hard to make ends meet, and was close to a financial breakthrough with the approach of a Master's Degree Graduation from a highly accredited University. Someone who didn't have a history of instability or irresponsibility and had no family support in the state at all. My family was close to 400 miles away. So, my response to the man was, "I don't have anywhere to go. Can they give me more time?" He said, "We can send you to the sister shelter down the street." While that was a "kind" gesture, most staff in that shelter knew that my soon-to-be ex-husband worked at the shelter down the street. The offer was insensitive and unsafe.

I'm so grateful for people like Tina and Jennifer (*names changed to protect their privacy*), who were single moms in their own right, both of them raising multiple children and both had also been through painful divorces. They each took me into their own homes a month apart from each other. So essentially, I lived with one of them for 30 days and the other one for 30 days. These strong Black Queens were my inspiration. They were holding their heads up, raising their children without support from their children's fathers, even though they had to cry some nights to do so. I didn't take their kindness for granted! I had used that time to knock on doors and bang on windows (*figuratively*) to get a place for me and my kids.

Having been so persistent in doing so, and not taking "no" for an answer: God blessed me to get into public housing in an unprecedented time frame of three months! I'll never forget the day I got the letter in the mail and what God had done the night before. I was at my wit's end emotionally and so overwhelmed. I had received a petition from Family Court as my estranged husband was threatening custody. However, his actions (or inaction regarding a "proposed reconciliation" once again encouraged by "*the church*") were a majority of the reasoning behind us ending up in a homeless shelter. The night before I received the letter about our new place, I was sitting on the edge of the bed in a gaze. My then 4-year-old son sat up in the bed and asked, "Mommy, what's wrong?"

"Nothing, son," I said. "Go back to sleep. Mommy just wishes we had our own place."

He said, "Don't worry, Mommy, we won't be here long." He was my little prophet! That very next day we received our letter telling us we were approved and giving us our new address!

Now, the public housing in rural areas is different from the public housing in the inner cities where I was raised. Not as notoriously dangerous and in better conditions if I was to compare. Yet, it's still public housing for me, and I didn't want to raise my kids in the "hood," but I was so grateful that God made a way! We moved into that apartment with help from some of the men from the church.

During our first couple of nights, I noticed the water smelled like eggs. So, I went out and bought bottled water, and we ate, drank, cooked, and bathed with it. I was not going to complain. I gave God thanks. I had also given away all my furniture except one couch and the kids' bunk bed. I was believing God for a new season! My hope was being renewed! I lay on the couch around that second or third night and said," God, I am so thankful for our new place. Please just don't forget I want to own my own house."

God had placed this scripture in my heart at that moment of my life:

Isaiah 43:19
See, I am doing a new thing!
Now it springs up; do you not perceive it?
I am making a way in the wilderness
and streams in the wasteland.

So, the day I was preparing to go in and officially meet my case manager and sign my lease, I heard God say to me, "Put on your business suit and bring your briefcase."

I was like, "Huh?" I didn't understand. I was going to sign a lease at a public housing office. Why was I getting dressed up in my business suit and bringing my briefcase for that? God didn't answer me; he repeated the statement. So, I obeyed his instructions.

I have learned that the greatest blessings come from acts of obedience! I remember walking into Mr. Alexander's office with a wave of confidence. It was the first time in so many years that I walked with my head held high like that and commanded a room! I said, "Mr. Alexander, I know I'm here to sign a lease, but I WANT TO OWN A HOUSE!"

I never sat down. He was looking up at me, and I was looking down at him! I was also wagging my finger and rolling my neck while talking to him. He smiled.

"I don't know what programs you have," I said, "But I want to own a house!"

He put his hand up like he was a crossing guard! He said, "OK! OK! Yes, we do actually have a program. Here are the criteria."

As I opened the brochure and read the bullet points describing the qualifications, I quickly discovered I didn't meet not one iota of them. But I walked out of Mr. Alexander's office with hope!

The next day, I remember leaving work and telling the Lord I was going to go to Walmart to purchase some decorations for my place and show him how much I appreciated him by fixing it up like it really was my *"house"* You know, those fancy curtain rods with the bling on each end? Yeah, those! So, I got all the way to Walmart, parked my car, and walked inside. When I got to the middle of the curtain aisle, I heard God say these words to me, *"Don't you buy nothing for that apartment because you're not gonna be there long."*

Now, first of all, let me explain something – I was the only person in the curtain aisle. That was the only item I went to the store to purchase. Like a slow-motion part of a movie, I turned around, stared into the air, and just slowly walked out. I mean, I laugh when I tell the story now. But it was so surreal. It was just me and God at that moment, and again, I obeyed.

Later that week, as I was returning home from work, I received a call from Mr. Alexander as I was putting the keys into my door to unlock it. He said, "Ms. Alishia, you made such an impression on us when you came to sign your lease; we just wanna PUT YOU in the homeownership program. Here are the addresses of the two houses we have. Go pick out which one you want and call me back."

I remember standing in the threshold of the doorway at that moment, looking around the living room's perimeter at all the boxes that I had not unpacked yet. That was still my first week in the apartment. I turned around and hurried back to my car!

"Lord, what is happening!" I said to myself. I had a flood of emotions: happy, excited, nervous. "Wait, Lord; this is the Housing Authority! *What these houses gonna look like!*" were my exact words.

I heard God say to me as I was practically speeding down the highway, "Don't despise small beginnings."

"Yes, Lord, " I humbly replied.

When I arrived at the first community, I can't say I liked it too much. So, I drove just a few more traffic lights south to the next neighborhood, and as I pulled into Briar Park in Camden, Delaware, and pulled up to what would be my very first home, I realized that, at that moment, I was experiencing God answering a very detailed prayer that I didn't even think was a prayer. You ever say something quietly to yourself, but you think it was just a thought? A wish even? I had "wished" that I could have a gray and black accented home. Well, this was a gray house with black shutters. I used to "wish" and daydream that I had a home with brick. Well, this was a gray and black home with red brick on the left side. HA! I remember just sitting in front of the house in my car, crying. I could see that they were doing some renovations to the home. It was on a nice little quiet end street, and there was nothing but an open field next to my home.

I picked out that house, and in two weeks, we went from moving into a public housing development and into my very own three-bedroom home that I would end up owning three years later. The housing authority would buy and renovate homes in the community and help their qualifying tenants through a Home Ownership program to become owners of those homes in a three-year timeframe. Shout out to Temeka Crawford, a woman of God sent by God to be my Housing Counselor, and in 2008, during a major housing crisis, I was going to settle on *my* home!

God used that journey to turn my pain into purpose! In 2004 my divorce was final; in 2005, I graduated from Wilmington University with my Master's Degree in Counseling, earning a 3.8 GPA, and having been inducted into the Chi Sigma Iota National Honor Society for aspiring Counselors. I launched my very own non-profit organization, Empowered Women Ministries, Inc. helping single women break cycles of unhealthy relationships, lead emotionally healthy lifestyles and live their purpose. We became international in 2015 and have served thousands of broken and hurting women across the United States and Jamaica, and St. Thomas through our programs: *Rebuilding Your Life After Divorce*™ and Single Sisters Empowered to L.I.V.E™. We even created a scholarship for single mothers in college giving away thousands of dollars. Lastly, we held an award ceremony for 7 years called: *The Empowered Women of the Year*™ *Award Ceremony*, honoring single mothers who had risen above adversity and achieved specific milestones in 5 categories, each resembling an area of my life God allowed me to excel in as a single mother!

In 2017, I established my own Real Estate business and, to date, have helped a little over 200 families to either become homeowners or transition from one home to the next. I have been blessed to sit at tables with widows, divorcing women, and single mothers and support them and represent them through one of the most difficult challenges of their lifetime while achieving one of the most rewarding goals, helping them to restore and renew their hope with the message of my story. God blessed me to go from below the poverty level to building a multi-million-dollar Real Estate business that has also trained and developed other real estate professionals nationwide. In 2009, God remembered me, just as he remembered Sarah, just as he remembered Rachel, just as he remembered Rebecca. But not with the birth of a new child, with the birth of a new marriage.

I met my purpose partner Randolph Potter, Jr, a man of prayer and an entrepreneur who was assigned to my life to love me as God loves his church and to help me raise our amazing, blended family! Our children are now college graduates in the medical and sports industries! God gave me beauty for ashes, and he can and WILL do the same for you! Don't despise your pain. Say yes to it. In saying yes to your pain, you are saying yes to a purpose beyond what you can see. Your pain will be the catalyst of the legacy you will leave on this earth. I don't want to go through what I went through ever again. I also would not change a thing. God said in Jeremiah 29:11 (MSG) I'll show up and take care of you as I promised.... I know what I'm doing. I have it all planned out—plans to take care of you, not abandon you, plans to give you the future you hope for.

ALISHIA POTTER

Alishia **Potter** is known as an atmosphere changer and fearless leader. She is passionate about using her 20+ years in the Education industry to help families build wealth and financial literacy through Real Estate. A Boston Native, and a master's level HBCU graduate, Alishia Potter is the owner and Team Leader of a multi-million dollar producing Real Estate Group called The Optimism Group at Keller Williams, servicing the DMV market. In 2021, she ranked as one of the top performers in the entire Maryland and DC Region of Keller Williams. She also ranks within the top 10% of agents within the Coastal Region. She was the first African American on the Eastern Shore of Maryland to hold a leadership position with the company, where she also served as one of the Ambassadors for the Social Equity Task Force, a national task force created by the Gary Keller, Founder of Keller Williams, after the murders of George Floyd, Breona Taylor, and Ahamud Arbery.

Alishia was also the first African American to be featured on a billboard in the real estate market on the Eastern Shore of Maryland in 2021, opening the doors for more people of color on the Eastern Shore to confidently grace the industry.

Her book: *Woman Will Thou Be Made Whole?* was published in 2007 and hit the international waves. Shortly after that, she published: *The Woman You've Empowered ME to Be! (2010)* Alishia launched a non-profit organization: Empowered Women Ministries, Inc, in 2008, which became international in 2015, launching her life-changing program: Rebuilding Your Life After Divorce and helping countless hurting and broken women heal and live empowered lives.

She is a domestic violence survivor, a breast cancer survivor, and a mental health conqueror who has embraced the power of tragedy to build a trajectory of destiny, purpose, and legacy. An ordained Elder in the Lord's church, Alishia enjoys serving in Pastoral care roles, serving the homeless community with her church's outreach department, and serving on the prayer team. She is a member of Union Church in Glen Burnie, Maryland.

She is also married to her purpose partner of 10 years, and they share the joy of having raised two young adult college graduates: Caleb and Sariah. A quote by Maya Angelou that she feels best describes how she lives her life is: *"If you're always trying to be normal, then you'll never know how amazing you can be."*

Facebook: Alishia Potter
LinkedIN: Alishia Potter
Instagram: @therealalishiapotter

Choose Joy In The Midst Of The Storm

By Tara Gilead-Johnson

I have a core group of friends who I cherish and share a lot of my life with. We bond over the simplest of life events to the most complex. Ryan was a part of my inner circle, my big brother from another mother. We started with me being his loctitian, and he was my client, but we became fast friends and spent 20-plus years being each other's lifeline. Ryan earned a front-row seat in my life. He had to give the nod to every boyfriend I had and was a confidant whose trusted advice I would always rely on. I never questioned his love or loyalty. When I purchased my first home, Ryan was there. When I changed jobs, Ryan was there. When life got tough, Ryan was there. Throughout my pregnancy, Ryan was there. When I moved across state lines, Ryan was there. When I got engaged and married, Ryan was there. When I did stupid things, Ryan was there to call me out and love me through whatever mess I made. When my aunt died, Ryan was there. When my mother-in-law died,

Ryan was there. He was there for my husband and son too. Ryan was always there. We were accountability partners for most things, and being the ambitious person I am, he was the keeper of my laundry list of goals. We laughed A LOT. That fool would crack a joke about everything, including things and people who should not be made fun of. He was kind and genuine with those he encountered. Ryan was a blessing to me in so many ways. He was that neutral voice of reason when my son misbehaved. He listened and had the ability to break things down in ways I could not. Some people illuminate the spaces they enter and melt the hearts of those around them. Ryan was that kind of person. He answered the phone every time I called, almost.

As 2019 was ending, I had high hopes for 2020 because it was the year that I would wholeheartedly chase my dreams without excuses, procrastination, abandonment, or delay. My son, at the time, was entering what he called "double digits," and I felt it was the ideal year to put my name back on the priority list. PERMANENTLY! I have never been a *resolution maker*, but I have BIG dreams and I am always working towards "something." I remember sitting in my childhood church on the last night of 2019, giving God all the glory for bringing me through all the ups and downs, peaks, and valleys. I asked God for 2020 to be a year I grew beyond the stagnation I was feeling. Frankly, I wanted to feel like myself again. I was ready to see 2019 end and take with it the pain and grief that I held for about ten months after watching my aunt Sony's decline and, ultimately, death. Cancer is such a bastard. I was tired of existing in a place of grief and sadness, so I wanted to shake the year off, pick up the pieces and watch God make beauty out of the ashes.

The clock struck midnight, and I felt the excitement of the new year. I felt hopeful that what was ahead of me was greater than what was behind me. The church buzzed with well wishes, hugs, tears, and laughter. Everyone, totally oblivious of the turmoil that would consume and, in many ways, change lives on a global scale, was in high spirits. Once I got to my childhood home and connected to Wi-Fi, I called Ryan. We expressed that traditional Happy New Year, but we quickly switched into planning mode, verbalizing the goals we wanted to accomplish. We made plans to invest in real estate, take trips, exercise, see each other often, hold each other accountable, support each other, and continue to be each other's ride-or-die. 2020 was going to be different because we were committed to progress. We had no idea how crazy 2020 was about to be.

March 2020 rolled around, and this thing called COVID 19, a mysterious illness at the time, that the world knew little about, annihilated my plans with quickness. Everything I wanted to accomplish that year was placed on the back burner. The days, weeks, and months that rolled into each other were filled with fear, misery, and bewilderment. I sanitized, cleaned, masked up, kept my distance from loved ones, and like the rest of the world, existed in a space of emotional anguish. I often cried while listening to the Governor at the time give news updates. The news of death tolls hitting thousands, toilet paper shortage, and body bags piling up in freezer trucks were frightening. I was worried that my husband, who graciously took on the responsibility of grocery shopping, would become exposed to the deadly COVID 19 and infect our home. I worried about my son, who is asthmatic, getting COVID-19. I felt overwhelmed about the future. I felt like I had no control over my life or choices because every choice could potentially be deadly. The isolation unraveled my emotional, physical, and mental well-being. I felt powerless. Sorrow devoured me, and a sense of hopelessness lingered like an unwelcome house guest.

Time passed. The death tolls continued to increase, and I was desperate yet again for another year to end. 2021 had to be better. I was cautiously optimistic because 2020, the year that began with great expectations, turned out to be a hot ghetto mess.

A few months into 2021, my mother-in-law became very ill. Really Jesus? Death, unhappiness, and illness hovered over us. Emotionally, I was depleted. Still navigating through the pandemic, my husband and I faced another trial. My husband was responsible for his mother's care for our entire relationship. He made sure she took her medication, prepared her meals, did her laundry, cleaned her home, monitored her health, and ensured that she stayed comfortable without help from his siblings. That was HARD. My husband loved his mother, and I admire that about him. My mother-in-law's health declined rapidly. How do you prepare yourself for the loss of a parent? Barely over the loss of my aunt, existing in the pandemic, and being thrust into being the support system for my husband as he prepared himself to say goodbye to his mother, well, that reduced every bit of strength I had. My mother-in-law passed away in October 2021. The season of sickness and darkness remained like a thick fog, suffocating us and sucking the joy from our hearts.

Our circle of friends and my family checked on us, ordered us meals, sent flowers, and cared for us. The village showed up, and for that, I am forever grateful. The morning of the funeral, my husband misplaced his keys, then he found them. Then he misplaced cards family members sent him to pass on to his brother and sister, then he found them. Then he had to check the door because he wasn't sure he locked it. Anxiety had him in a loop, trying to delay the inevitable. Compassionate, although anxious myself, I called Ryan. To our surprise, he and his wife drove to NY the night before to attend the funeral service. I told my husband, and just like magic, he found the clarity and strength he needed to get on the way. Ryan and his wife sat next to us during the service; both were the shoulders we leaned on the entire time. Their presence made me feel comforted. My husband was so brave and strong, but deep down, losing his mother hurt. The weeks after my mother-in-law's passing, Ryan checked on us frequently, especially my husband.

November 8, 2021, was a beautiful fall day. It was cool for that time of year; the sun was bright, and the sky was cloudless and blue. The perfect weather and, oddly, the day felt magical. It was as if God was giving us a gift of peacefulness at that moment because He is all-knowing. After weeks of misinformation and the funeral home blaming COVID for the delayed delivery of the death certificate, it was finally ready for pickup. My husband and I hopped in the truck and headed on our way. We didn't say much on the way there. We listened to the radio, and I sang along to whatever was playing. We pulled into the parking lot. Remembering the last time, I was there, I told my husband, Ryan, blocked traffic on the day of the funeral to give me a chance to exit the lot. If you know anything about New York drivers and traffic, you understand. Only Ryan could block traffic without getting cussed out. Surprisingly no one honked, and I was able to ease out of the lot without incident. It was the first time I shared that with my husband, and he mentioned how much it meant to him that Ryan and his wife drove eight hours round trip to stand with us in such a difficult moment.

On our way home from picking up the death certificate, the energy changed. While the sky was still blue and the sun bright, our emotions were choking us. The sadness was thick, and I could tell my husband was on the verge of tears, so I did what was natural for me. I called Ryan. As I said before, he always picked up my calls.

"Gilhead, what ah gwarn?" I rolled my eyes as if he could see me and responded like I did for the last 20 years.

"Boy, you better learn how to say my name."

At the time, Ryan, his wife, his brother, his sister-in-law, and another couple were in Puerto Rico for a pre-birthday trip. Ryan's 47th birthday was coming up on November 28, and his brother's birthday would have been November 17th. Both, along with their partners and friends, were living it up, enjoying the island life. They were in "vacation turn up" mode. Unknown to Ryan, his wife was planning a surprise birthday party for him.

The venue was booked, and the pieces falling into place. Our group chat was filled with the details of the event, and frankly, after the emotional roller coaster of losing my mother-in-law, a good party was right on time. The conversation, which will be forever etched in my memory, was good. We laughed HARD, talked about working out, bike riding, and just being our silly selves. Almost immediately, the somber mood shifted, and the calmness returned. Ryan said that we should get back into our workout routine after the holidays. I agreed. We told each other I love you and hung up. The day felt easy after that. I had a good conversation with my friend. God truly is all-knowing, and the events following validate this fact even more.

I am somewhat competitive; I play games, I know I can win, and play against those I can beat. Punk move, but I am who I am. If I can't win, I am not playing. Knowing Ryan agreed to start working out after the holidays, I had to "one up" him and get started before him. He was on vacation, with the conversation about working out fading into a distant memory. Tuesday, November 9, was my official start date. I got through the workday, dropped my son off to Jujitsu, and quickly laced up my sneakers to jump on the treadmill. I had not been on the treadmill in weeks, so it was an utter surprise that I was hitting my 75th run. Not only was I ahead of Ryan, all of a sudden, I had extra bragging rights.

After my run, I recorded a video being the loudest and doing the most. I sent the video to our group chat to taunt Ryan, and within seconds the phone rang. I picked up with the same energy I sent the video. I was hollering and showing off. The voice on the other end was Ryan's wife, and her gut cry caught me completely off-guard. Since it was a group chat, the phone rang to all parties, so my husband picked up as well.

I heard, "Tara, they didn't make it; they got caught."

My brain tried to make sense of what I was hearing; however, I could not. The wailing on the other end confirmed something was terribly wrong, but somehow, I did not have the capacity to pull together the words being communicated to me. Then I heard another gut-wrenching cry, and "No! No! No! No!" This time it was my husband's voice.

I was very confused. I recall feeling internal chaos and hearing unnatural cries, but I could not move. I was so confused. My feet and body felt weird. What was happening? Time stood still. As an emotional intelligence coach, I am present with my emotions. I can identify my feelings and label and address them. Sadly, in the moments following sending that taunting workout video, that skillset was failing miserably.

I could not understand what Ryan's wife was saying or why my husband was looking at me like he was. Perhaps I was having an out-of-body experience, but nothing in the moment felt familiar. I suddenly felt fear. Deep fear. I flopped on the stairs. Literally flopped. I managed to sit up for a moment.

My brain held the words, "They got caught," and my lips released. "They got caught doing what?"

If I am honest, I think getting caught doing something was an easier reality for me to accept. They got caught doing what? Running a stop light? Ryan nor his brother were involved in illegal activities, so what did they get caught doing? The fearful feeling was replaced with annoyance. I was going to kick Ryan's behind if he got caught up in mess that caused such emotional cries. What the H...?

In between sobs, Ryan's wife explained the best she could the tragedy which occurred. She repeated, "They didn't make it."

I cut her off, almost being belligerent. "They didn't make what? Got caught doing what?"

Almost as if she was trying to avoid saying exactly what happened because saying the words would somehow further confirm what she knew.

Sobbingly she said, "Tara, they drowned."

Confused, I asked, "They who?" She could NOT be saying what I thought. There was no way that Ryan was included in the "they" that drowned. Did she mean drowned as in dead?

A zillion thoughts were colliding into an incomprehensible mental mess. Reality kicked my butt hard. I hung up the phone. I do not remember saying goodbye, but I had to call Ryan. His number is permanently etched in my memory even now. It's one of the only phone numbers I know by heart. He was also in my favorites, but there I was fumbling, looking for a phone that was already in my hand. I called Ryan, but he did not answer. I called him again. Three times. He did not answer. No, that's not supposed to happen. He always answers my calls. Why didn't he answer? Wait, what time was it? We needed to leave to pick up our son from Jujitsu. What is happening? I had many random thoughts, and I was barely able to hold myself up. My husband cried. I bawled.

I had to cancel a meeting, and I also needed to leave the house. Jujitsu was over. I canceled my meeting, and expressing the reason behind my cancellation was surreal. "Hey, I can't meet because my brother and his brother drowned."

Then I called my mother; it was at that point I completely lost it. Mama Linky, as Ryan called my mother, was shocked to hear the news. I heard my mother say, "Ryan? Dead? How is that possible?"

How did we go from the perfect Monday, where Ryan was alive and well, to 24 hours later, he was dead? In the blink of an eye!

Having to tell a child, someone he loves, died is horrific. The Saturday prior, my son spoke with Ryan, who was his godfather, about his soccer game. He wasn't in the greatest of moods because his team lost.

Ryan listened and told him the main goal was to have fun. While my son heard what his godfather said to him, he was still pissed that his team had lost. That conversation was four days prior. I was an emotional wreck, sobbing uncontrollably and trying to explain to my former manager that I could not attend work the next day. I was snotty, salty, messed up, and broken.

My husband went into the center and being weepy, he told our son that something bad happened. He entered the car and asked, "Mom, what's wrong?"

He heard me talking to my manager and later told me he thought that I was crying because I got fired. God knows, I wish being fired was the reason I was bawling instead of mourning the tragic death. How would a child make sense of this tragedy? I whispered; your uncle Ryan died. I couldn't even look at my son. I had nothing to give him at that moment and as his mother I felt terrible guilt. The pain shattered my heart. I was grieving for my son, whom I could not console after hearing the worst news; I was grieving for my husband, who was dealing with the loss of his mother, which was compounded times two with Ryan's passing. I was grieving for Ryan's wife, his children, and his parents. Oh God, his parents lost two children at the same time. I was grieving for Ryan. His life was cut short, taking away his sweet spirit from this earth.

That night, my husband, my son, and I slept in the same bed. Refusing to separate and choosing to console each other through everything that had turned our world upside down. Days following, we spoke only when necessary, and we cried often. I was a shell of a woman.

The news spread quickly through the Caribbean community and in the DMV, bringing sorrow and grief to everyone who knew them. The drowning of two brothers in Puerto Rico while on vacation replayed on news stations, and the story was everywhere. Social media was flooded with tributes. We intended to travel to Maryland for a surprise birthday party, but in the blink of an eye, the event changed to a double funeral. How? Why?

Those close to Ryan remembered how kind-hearted and generous he was, always putting others before himself without expecting anything in return. Even though it seemed impossible for anyone to move on after such a tragedy, people began paying tribute by organizing candlelight vigils while also offering support for his grieving family and loved ones. There was standing room only at the funeral for Ryan and his brother. The line to view the bodies was miles long, with some being turned away. The tragedy ripped my heart to pieces. Their birthdays, Thanksgiving, Christmas, and every holiday following felt strange and empty.

I am never going to forget that phone call. My best friend, my brother, the person whom I loved unconditionally and who loved me, was gone. He died tragically, and no amount of wishing could have changed that. I was heartbroken and angry. While I was in my own sea of grief, I had to suck it up to be strong for my husband, my son, and Ryan's wife.

I wallowed in self-pity and tears. I wanted my friend to be alive and knowing that wouldn't ever happen made the sadness linger. My nights and days were spent consoling my husband and Ryan's wife. I was the ear to vent to, the shoulder they needed to lean on. Life doesn't have a "pause" button, so I still had to parent, do dishes, clean up, work, run errands, and show up bravely when weak was all I cared to be.

I needed rest but got very little of it. I needed sleep, but Ryan's wife needed me more. I needed stillness, but my husband's heart ached, so I couldn't dare be still. I was in emotional turmoil. My son needed his mother, and I had to be available for him. My heart was broken, and I was angry. Ryan was taken away, and I was not prepared. Memories of him made me cry, angry, bitter, and resentful. But something miraculous happened – one day, while sitting in my closet, looking at pictures of Ryan, the Holy Spirit reminded me that weeping endures in the night, but joy comes in the morning. A voice echoed in my subconscious as if I had spoken the words out loud. If there was ever going to be hope for me amidst this grief, then it would have to come from Jesus Christ and His infinite love for me.

God reminded me that if I wanted to heal, I had to be intentional. I had to make a choice to feel something in addition to the sadness or instead of the gloom. I was reminded that joy did not "just happen." I had to choose to joy every single day. Despite missing Ryan deeply each day, somehow, those painful moments became easier. I leaned into God more and allowed myself to let go of the pain. It was the only way I was going to survive losing a piece of my heart.

Experiencing death, sadness, and uncertainty consistently for over four years taught me many lessons about myself. From a healed place, I recognize that I could be more intentional about my expressions of love. While I told my loved ones I loved them, I realized that I did not say it often enough nor show it as much as I should have. Grief showed me that I could not take people for granted, and sadly I had to lose loved ones for that lesson to wedge deep within. I cheated myself and my family of my time and energy. I worked more hours than I should have at times when that time should have been spent being present with family. I also learned that I needed to be kinder to myself and lower my expectations. I am way too hard on myself, and I have at times, set unrealistic expectations for myself. That needed to stop. Healing has opened a pathway for me to extend myself grace and gratitude.

Death and loss created a mirror that showed me a reflection that I needed to change. I walked through the season of heartache and feeling like I would not make it. Healing has proven otherwise. I completely surrendered to God during the darkest hours of my life, and laying at his feet has restored me. God touched my heart and gave me peace. God touched my mind and overhauled my thinking. I pray more and worry less. Nothing I endured happened to me. Instead, they happened **for** me. I had to go through the fire so I could stand up in victory. Tough times don't last, but tough people do. I am Built God Tough, and my experiences have validated that.

Trusting in God isn't always easy, but it's essential to living a fulfilling life. Trusting God brings peace, improves relationships, gives us purpose, and requires us to surrender control. By developing trust in God through prayer, reading, and meditation, we can tap into a source of wisdom and strength that will guide us through hardship. As a child of God, I am confident I have unlimited access to a power greater than myself that would help me navigate even the most difficult circumstances. God gives us hope!

TARA GILEAD-JOHNSON

Tara Gilead-Johnson is an International Best-Selling Author. She is a Certified Life Coach – specifically certified as an Emotional Intelligence Coach and an active member of the internationally recognized Certified Coaches Alliance. She is a working mother, wife, entrepreneur, believer in the Gospel of Jesus Christ, and a dope island girl who believes in the power of community. Hailing from the island of Antigua, she LOVES music, warm sunny days, and traveling, and she "might" commit a crime for milk chocolate. She has a son, the light of her life, the beat of her heart, the drive behind her ambitions, and a husband who is her soulmate. They live in the empire state – NY. With so many responsibilities, Tara is very intentional about the boundaries she has in place to maintain the balance between home and work. Her No means No, and her Yes means Yes. Respect that!

You can connect with Tara on
Facebook @ Tara Gilead-Johnson or
www.taragileadjohnson.com

The Lion's Den
by Myeisha Scofield

The Lion's Den was my rock bottom. I was in a place where everything I faced had one job; **to take me out of here**! I was meant to be defeated; I was meant to be destroyed. What I came out as was **changed.** I came out unscathed from the traps the devil had set up for me. Rock bottom placed me closest to God in those moments. I was facing full-on destruction, mentally and also physically.

See, before I went into the Lion's Den, I was journeying through the jungle. By the jungle, I mean the things of this world that separate you from God. I was fighting a battle against myself. I struggled with fully accepting who I was and who I was to become. I was lost out in that jungle. I was lusting after a love that was never meant to be. I was stuck in a seasonal moment and trying to make it a lifetime. Back then, I couldn't see myself blocking my blessings. I thought I knew better than God. All the time, I was being given opportunities to leave this situation, and I would not. But I know a God that sits high and looks low. I was devastated at the time, but what happened was done.

There was no way I was letting this man go. Two black eyes later, it became very clear. No matter how much I thought I wanted this relationship, there was no way I could move forward with this man—never had a man put his hands on me or beat me up, for that matter. This was supposed to be my wake-up call.

I accepted the apology and went back. I still was not supposed to be there. So, God intervened once more. This time it was in the form of my car being repossessed. As we were sitting, laughing, joking, and watching tv late at night, we heard a loud noise. Upon checking, the towing company had come to repossess my car. Not only was I now without a car miles away from civilization, but the rent was also behind, and the electric company had sent a cut-off notice. Seemed like everything that could happen was doing so right before my eyes. By the next day, he had decided that he was moving back home, and ultimately, I also had to move to another town. I felt alone, I felt abandoned, I felt isolated, I felt stupid, and I felt very low. This was the end of the road for us. This was the end of this toxic chapter. I could not help myself for wanting to reopen it; I didn't want to close it out; I never wanted to admit the defeat and failure I felt behind it all. I didn't want to let him go. I could love him; we could make it work, right? Yeah, he hit me, but he was sorry. All the things I knew were all wrong, I ignored. Who had I become? Working with battered women, and here I had gotten battered. I was so ashamed. Yet I still wanted him back.

The move from where I was to Salisbury was my new beginning. At first, I could not appreciate it. I missed my toxic love. I was moving on but still holding on to hope that this mess would work out. Months had gone by; I shed all the tears I could. I had moved my son and me in with my brother. I threw myself into caring for my son, spending all my time with him, pouring into him. I didn't like it or understand it, but this was exactly where we were meant to be. God blocked me from a situation I continued trying to put myself in. He saved me from myself.

After finally accepting that we had to part ways, it was then that I began to go within. The damage had been done. I was still lost, searching for answers, waiting to hear the voice of God. It was this time that strengthened me. It was at this time that I felt I could tell God the plans I had for me. I wanted to tell him how angry I was that things hadn't worked out. I felt like he got it all wrong! This was my soulmate, my person, my best friend, right? WRONG! He busted my bubble right then! I was waiting to hear a word from him, but it was silent. If he was going to show me what his plan was for me, I would have to listen; I would have to humble myself before him!

I had said all I had to say and was ready to hear his direction, or so I thought. He wasn't speaking to me. Everything was quiet. My thoughts were silent; his voice was silent. I was inside The Lion's Den. In real life, this was a walk-in closet I had claimed as my own. I stayed there; I slept there; I prayed there. This time, when everything was quiet, was where I gained peace of mind, where I was able to heal the broken pieces of my heart. It took some time, but in these dark, quiet moments, I rebuilt myself. In those solitaire moments, I found myself. I found myself happy and content with me. I found myself loving me more. I found real peace and was still able to pick back up. I found a deep true love for me from myself. I would never allow myself to lose sight of who I was or where I was going ever again.

Daniel 6: 16-18
"Early the next morning, the king rushed to The Lions' Den. He called to Daniel to see if he was still alive. Daniel called back! He told the King that God sent an Angel to shut the lions' mouths. The lions did not hurt him."

It felt like all of the odds were stacked against me. I had lost EVERYTHING! Just when it began looking like I had lost it all, I had an epiphany. None of this was a loss. What was gone had to go! I lost feelings of loneliness; I lost feeling inept; I healed. In all that I lost, what I gained was so valuable. None of my experiences were meant to hurt me. God had already sent an Angel to protect me from all that was sent to destroy me. I had to go through all of this to get to the next level in my journey. We all have dens in our lives filled with lions ready to rip us to pieces. This is my testimony! God will not let what the enemy sends destroy you. I am Built God Tough, and so are you! You are a force; you are chosen; you were built for this life.

God finally spoke to me. He showed me in a dream my light; it was shining from my hands. He said I was given this light to heal myself and others. I had to go through it all to find a purpose in all the mess I had allowed myself to go through. I pray that his light shines through me to touch each of you.

BUILT GOD TOUGH

Dark in the Lion's Den, I barely could see
Yet I came out unharmed, God saved me
From the mouth of the beast, to devour me whole
God restored my heart and mind, he saved my soul
I was built for this life, it's why I'm so tough
I stand on his promises, I know I am enough
All along I didn't know his plan
But never did he let go of my hand
At my lowest I thought I lost it all
It was then he gave me the courage to stand tall
He built me God tough, like a warrior Queen
Tough exterior but sweeter than I seem
A woman of God with vision, and a dream

MYEISHA SCOFIELD

Myeisha Scofield is a native of Denton, MD. She is a writer by nature and has been writing for 27 years. Myeisha discovered her love for writing at 12 when she wrote her first poem. Now she is writing books! Myeisha is a self-published author. Her fiction novel "Honeysuckle Summer" released in October 2022 on amazon. Myeisha is owner and CEO of East 11 T Shirt Company which she started in 2021 behind a passion for graphic design and t shirts. Myeisha is a mother to 4 amazing boys: Michaelen, Sincere, Micah and Messiah.

myeishascofield.com

Survivor Of God's Fittest

By Crystal Brinson

As we come into the world, you never expect to go through journeys that are not quite pretty, interrupted, or harsh. Survivor is a technique that God puts into each of us to overcome the test we go through. According to the Merriam-Webster dictionary, Survivor of the fittest is defined as the natural process by which organisms best adjusted to their environment are most successful in surviving and reproducing (2023).

My definition of Survivor of God's Fittest is overcoming the test that God proves every time that we are overcome by testimonies in situational conditions that is uncontrolled by the journey of life. In 1980 of September God began the test of my life's journey. Even then, the test began with a different type of test, the test of love by your parents. At the beginning of a child coming into a world, there is happiness and joy, but never do believe that it only lasts for a segment of life that would change the rest of the adult journey. My mother was excited because I was the miracle that survived her pregnancy.

My father was excited, but the shift will change in the next events of this life span. Being raised by a single mother tends to have other important people in your life like a mom mom (grandmother), pop pop (grandfather), aunts, and uncles with different personalities, but they were the family that I learned to love and embrace. In this story, my relationship with my father constantly changed, which will show the survivor that I endured until deliverance took place. As a child while my mother was at work, a family kept trying to have intercourse with me, but in some kind of way, umm, God helped me through this ugly journey. The crazy part is that I suppressed this memory until I was twenty-three years old. After a tragic moment in life, the memory came forth.

Five years later, after not seeing my father, he finally came to get me due to a court order. Then he spends money on me but drops me off with his girlfriend at the moment. We consider this pattern happened every visit unless there is a special reason to spend time with just me and him. I did not overcome this test until 2023 when I decided not to allow toxic people to control my life anymore. I am jumping ahead, so let me slow down. In school, I was a really tiny, skinny little girl that did not fit in with the in-crowd but fought to try to be a part of groups that did not match my character. Right then is when I first heard God tell me the direction of life. Now we call this a prophetic gift, but I was just hearing a voice at the time. The voice would tell me not to do things or give me directions, but I thought I was crazy, but never did I share this with anyone. I was going to church then, but I did not understand half of what the preacher was talking about because I was just tired of being in church.

Throughout my school journey, I would try to be seen going to different school activities that would prove that I was a leader, but all the time was a follower in nature, just wanting to be accepted. Meanwhile, my stepfather came onto the scene. I was happy because he was awesome, but I would always treat him as such because I wanted Daddy's love from my daddy. I watched how he would treat my sister and brother, but I wondered why he did not love me like them. I am a middle on his side, but on my mommy's side, I was her only child. Even the love of my family, because I had a strong family on my mother's side that treated me like a little princess, there was a void that I could not shake. Looking back, I was ungrateful because I had an awesome family, and God replaced the void with a stepfather, but I wanted my daddy.

Dating was by far the worst; I put myself in a terrible relationship to fill the void of daddy instead of having God send me to love the right way.

High school was by far the worst when it came to relationships until my senior year. By now, my best friend in the world had passed away the year of my graduation, which was my mom mom. When I tell you the worst; it was the worst feeling of my life. It was times I wanted to kill myself in high school because of boys not wanting me, but now I realize it was me putting me in places in my life that should not be. I pressured them to fill a void and not have a relationship. I met in my senior year an army soldier that blew my mind. He was so courteous to me that he kissed my hand when first met him; I did not let him know, but Lord, I sold. His name was Reuben, but they called him Dj but never I would ever think he would be my husband today. I thought God, you did this for me. I am so happy. The issue with Dj was he was in the Army in Texas, and I am in Maryland, but our friendship keeps the fire of relationship till this day. I was so sad when he had to go back, but I kept in contact with him.

I finally graduated, but not the way most people do. I graduated in summer school because my teacher failed me by two points, so I was not able to walk with my class. I was so embarrassed that I could not face anybody for a very long time. What was crazy was that my dad came to graduation like the proud parent he was, but really, he did not have a love for me. I never even spoke of it to my children or my husband until my son's senior year of high school. At this point, I was working on saving money so I could go to Texas to see my man, so I thought. I told Mom I was going to Texas to see my man, and she said, "No, you're not." I was like, Mom, I am grown now and graduated. What's the problem she said, "No, you not going." So, a little later, I told Dj I could not come, but that did not stop me.

I enlisted in the Army; Mom said I needed to do something because I was not going to college. Now nobody knew that I had dyslexia, but I knew something was wrong, but I never said anything. So, I could have gone to college, but I knew I was going to waste

174

money. Plus, I was joining the military to get my man, or so I thought.

I am heading to Ft. Jackson, South Carolina, to get to basic training excited because I think I am grown, no longer by the rules of mommy, and I will see my man. Nope, heading straight to, yelling, rushing me to eat, and running all day. I never speak badly about the military as a whole because this journey taught me to stand up for myself, my character, and my strength. Now I am not going to say that I didn't complete basic training; just know the weeks before heading to Advance Individual Training (AIT), I took sick, which caused me to not graduate on time. My dad showed up for graduation with my other family to find out that I did not walk. Weeks later, I passed my examination and headed to Ft. Lee, Virginia, three hours away from home. Could I say I was hyped that I get to see my family on weekends? Dj was on my mind, but I was focused on getting through this and then finding him. When I tell you the shock of all came when I got to Ft. Lee, it did just that. So, I got to see some of my friends that I should graduate with, but they were partying. I was getting screamed at again because I had a new drill sergeant who wanted to make a point. When I tell you we clashed, we did just that; she smoked me so bad that I had a headache for over three days. I called home crying to Mom to come to get me. I quit, so she would encourage me not to give up. As I was down in Ft. Lee, we were able to get passes to go off post or walk free on a post by having a curfew which I could have.   I started going to the club for soldiers on post, and suddenly I started going with one of my classmates from basic training. We dated for a while going different places, but he wanted to pressure me to have sex, and honestly, I hated sex. I did not know why at the time but didn't like it. Now with Dj, it was a totally different experience, but I was not trying to do this with anybody else. So, we broke up; one day, we were in cooking class when a light-skinned man walked up to me asking my name; I thought he was crazy. He introduced himself and told me he was a holdover, like I knew what it meant. His unit was beside mine, but I was still cautious because I knew I wanted Dj more than anybody. We dated for the for-rest time there. Finally, I might move on from Dj, but if I'll enjoy the fun for now.

I dated him until my order came up for Hawaii; I called him because then he was out of AIT, and he was in the National Guard, so he went back home to North Carolina. I call him one day which put the needle in the haystack for me; a woman's voice say hello. I was nervous, but I asked for him she immediately said, "What do you want with my husband?"

Tears fell down my face, but I said, "Ma'am, I did not know he was married, and I dated him while training. I am sorry for this."

She told me it was okay, but I got something for him. My attitude went from happy to rage. In a still voice, I heard, "Wipe the tears and get ready to go to Hawaii."

My mommy came down to my graduation. I did not invite anybody else because I did not want to disappoint them if I did not walk due to something happening. I graduated on time, smiling ear to ear. My mom took me home so that I could spend time with her before I headed to Hawaii.

I enjoyed my time with her, and we headed to the airport to drop me off; my mother gave me the advice and tips I needed. I left Maryland to head to Hawaii. A fresh new start, so I thought; I got the reception they gave me my location. So far, so good. Here comes, this guy coming to talk to me.

Immediately I was irritated because he was another clown coming to waste my time. He was so smooth that he reminded me of Dj, but as always, I struggled with the fact that I wanted to fill a void. After a rough break up after a month, I went through surgery, and the doctor told my mom and me that I couldn't have kids. I was so blown, but I just said, "Oh well," never knew that during my surgery, there was a surprise of a lifetime.

I came home to visit my family, I kept getting sick, and my aunt kept saying, "You gained weight."

I always flew nine hours on a plane getting back and forth to Hawaii, but this flight was horrible. I was nauseous the whole trip. Still, I did not think it was anything to be concern about, so I went to the doctor when I got back. The surprise of a lifetime came to full tuition. I am pregnant...I was so happy but sad because it was by a man I did not want to be involved with. However, my best blessing came into the world nine months later. I was happy as I could be. Now the whole time, I never told my family but my mother, aunt, and my son's Godmother. I went through ups and downs with my son's dad, so it was time for me to get out of the Army. My void, I thought, was gone, but it soon came to realize it is not gone.

Back in Maryland, by this time, I am going through a mental issue due to post-traumatic stress disorder (PTSD), but I am a single mother with a handsome son. I went through a rough point in my life because I was clubbing and running from God. I would attend church, but I did not want to be in church. I wanted to do me. I went through men like it was water, uncle this and uncle that. So, I reached out to my father for help, especially when my car was in a car wreck.

It did not last because he came and got the car back, but I was not surprised. I would try to reconnect with my father over the years, even trying to involve my son in his life, but there was a disconnect. I moved away to turn right back to come home due to having a mild TIA due to birth control path with assorted other things going on.

Now there are more grandchildren in my dad's life, but I noticed there was a generational curse which is favoritism in grandchildren, which my son was not the favorite. I got upset because I now see the same thing happening as it did to me. I nipped in the bud as soon as possible, but my mom addressed my dad because when she said something, he would listen to me. Here comes another blessing in my life: my daughter, whom I thought I was good now. I am the only child that had a girl. Dad is going to be in my life for sure. He was, but he started to be favoring her over my son. I stopped that before it got worst.

At this point, I am back in church and healing from different areas of life I lack. Now after eighteen years, I am marrying the love of my life Dj. Now I wanted to be Godly to have both of my dad's walk me down the aisle. My biological dad was mad about it, so I decided to let my son walk me down because I didn't want to let him down. Later, I found out he was mad because I put in my wedding program my mom and stepfather, then him like he was the stepfather, he felt. This is not the case, but I let it go because it is foolish. As the years went by, I don't really fool with my dad, but he took ill, so I came to the hospital to support him through everything. The next thing I know, he is back talking down to me again. I was like; I am totally done now.

Some more years go by, but I would call and check on my father from time to time because I am on the Christian journey of growing. So, I contacted him again to help me get another vehicle because my car was getting ready to go up. He and I went looking together. I thought he was going act like a dad was supposed to, but that was not the case. The whole time of helping me, he taunted me with a lecture or put me down. I had a deal to get at the car dealer, but he was going back and forth with help. Mommy stepped in as always and explained she knew how to handle this. She just needs a vehicle. The next day I was taking my daughter to school, and he explained to me that he felt I had an attitude, and I wouldn't be disrespected. My daughter started crying because he was yelling at me. Once I got her straight, I dropped off my bonus daughter and had to go back to meet him. I finally snapped, which was not my intention because I was raised to honor thy mother and father in my days in Exodus 20:12. However, parents forget don't provoke their child to wrath (Ephesians 6:4). This was not a proud moment, and I repented numerous times from incident.

I graduated from community college, and my son graduated from high school as I promised him. Then transferred to full colleges and graduated with my bachelor's degree from two different colleges with two majors. The little girl who has dyslexia and tried to fit in from Princess Anne, Maryland, has accomplished so much. My dad attended my graduation, and he said, "I am so proud of you", those words were the best I ever heard after 41 years of my life.

However, as before, he changed again.

This time I made a stop at the revolving door. God blessed me with an awesome stepfather or replaced the void. Why am I giving energy to a negative situation? I am not a little girl anymore who craves her daddy's love. I go one step further. God has been my daddy from the beginning when I was created in my mother's womb (Psalms 139:16). In 2023, at the age of 42, I finally got delivered from the void that haunted me for all those years. Will God mend the relationship? Only God knows, but I do know this I am beautiful and wonderful, made by him (Psalms 139:14). No matter what, he loves me, and that love is unconditional.

I am Built God Tough because God created me to be the woman of God that is loved by him.

"Survival of the fittest." *Merriam-Webster.com Dictionary, Merriam-Webster,* https://www.merriam-webster.com/dictionary/survival%20of%20the%20fittest. Accessed 23 Apr. 2023.

CRYSTAL BRINSON

Crystal Brinson has been called Advocate for people that God sends her way. She has a special love for children, youth, and preteens on loving themselves despite what life journeys bring. She became an ordained Prophetess of the Gospel in December 2022, being a woman of great change in her life. Learning that life is not just rainbows and unicorns, Crystal loves people beyond themselves. Overcoming adversity but knowing her faith in God will get her through any storms. Crystal currently works in the school systems where she advocates for all components which consist of the administrators, staff, students, families, and community. Being a wife, daughter, mother, Suga Mom, GiGi, and Ya Ya to name a few titles she carries. Currently, a grad student in Social Work after graduating she is pursuing a Doctor of Social Work (DSW).

Being not accepted or black sheep help Crystal becomes the woman she has become. Having a past that was not always acceptable to man but knowing God loves her just the way she was created. Wanting the world to be perfect in an imperfect world helps her grow strength to better herself. Having the courage to be a leader in different avenues in my childhood that continues in adulthood. Remember that at the end of the day what God feels is what matters not man. Learning that her beauty is not just outside but inside as well. Gaining confidence in who and whom she belongs to.

Connect with Crystal Brinson
14mrsbrinson@gmail.com
Facebook: Crystal Brinson
IG: CrystalTynell80

My Weakness is His Strength
By Jennifer Penick

I know that I am 'Built God Tough' because I was born fighting. That's right, from the moment I was born, I had to fight just to breathe. There were times in my young life when I felt no one had to fight harder to live than I did. I came into this world premature with underdeveloped lungs. There were many symptoms and even more treatments, but it all boiled down to one word, ASTHMA! Asthma threatened to take me out before I could fulfill my purpose on earth; before I could dance, jump rope, or climb a tree; before I could have a party and dance the night away; before I could be in love or see the world. Yes, asthma was trying to stop me before I could live and enjoy all that this life had to offer. I wanted to have children. I wanted in my heart not to be sick at all. I wanted to be able to breathe, to walk, to run, to skip, to jump, to dance, and I wanted it all without the FEAR of having an asthma attack.

I am able to share this testimony with you 44 years later because God is GOOD! He developed my lungs, my will to fight, and my ability to control my breathing by calming my mind. Every single day I got stronger and stronger in my fight. Today, I'm a full-blown WARRIOR! I am more capable, more confident, and more courageous than I ever thought I would be. So many times, in my life, I thought I would never get to where I am now. It's sad to say, but I never thought that I would live this long.

I thought asthma would take me out. I thought that word that I could not even spell would prevent me from living a full and active life. I suffered from anxiety and depression because there were times when living with asthma didn't feel like living at all. Nothing but God kept me here. God kept sending medications and medical personnel to revive me and to help me breathe. The more that I continued to live, the more I began to realize that God was saving me for a reason. The more that I lived, the more I understood that God was allowing me to have this disease so that I could overcome it so that I could fight it, so that I could show myself and the world exactly how strong I really was. To God be the glory!

God made me tough by allowing me to be weak. My illness impacted many areas of my life, but it never stopped me from being like all the other kids. I fought asthma daily to have a life that was filled with activity, travel, and DANCE! Battling chronic asthma taught me that I could overcome circumstances by fighting to get better and never giving up. I decided that I would not succumb to my diagnosis. I would not sacrifice the ability to run or ride a bike or dance simply because it became a challenge to breathe. I decided that if I needed that inhaler, I would use it, although I really hated using it. I was determined to show up for myself, and I was determined to be as strong as God always told me I could be.

His scripture says in Isaiah 41:10:
"Fear not, for I am with you. Be not dismayed, for I am your God. I will strengthen you. I will help you. I will uphold you with my righteous right hand."

I finally got to a point in my life where asthma no longer posed a daily risk. I had learned to manage my activities and my medication to the point where I controlled my asthma; my asthma did not control me.

It's sometimes difficult to trust in God's plan when we don't know how he's going to bring us through a certain situation and how we are going to overcome our challenges, especially the ones that have been with us for as long as we can remember. I encourage you to look to the struggles and challenges that God gives you that are out of your control and see how you can master those things so that they do not prevent you from living the life that God has purposed you to live.

When I was young, God showed me that I would dance. He showed me that I would love fitness and exercise and be healthy. When I got to a point in my life as an adult that I didn't see those things reflected in my life, I knew that I had made choices that were out of alignment with the will of God. The first thing I had to do to live the life that God had shown me was to get right with God. I had to start intentionally revealing myself to God in a way I had never done before. When I finally started having real conversations with myself, and God, God helped me understand who I was made to be and how I had gotten to this place in life. God is so great and gracious that he showed me how to get back in alignment with his will. God helped me to start by saying "NO" to the version of me that did not fit who and what God created me to be. Then, I started taking daily steps to say "YES" to the version of me that I knew lived on the inside. On the inside, I was just a girl that wanted to be a great mom, daughter, sister, friend, and loved one. That version of myself just wanted to be loved and accepted, and she was fighting and begging to be FREE. I had covered her with so many layers of versions of me that weren't me at all. Those other versions were just who I felt I needed to be to show up in the world and be okay. To show up in the world and not feel sick and weak and unable to breathe.

God strengthened me inside and out and made me see that I am so much more than the way I show up in the world and that I can always show up in the world as exactly who God made me to be, and that's BUILT GOD TOUGH!!!

JENNIFER PENICK

Jennifer Penick is an extraordinary Bestselling Christian author and mother of three smart and talented boys. As a mental health professional for the past 20 years, Jennifer has dedicated her life to helping others, particularly young people, find hope, healing, and purpose in their lives. While providing mental health services in the African American community, Jennifer witnessed the transformative power of faith in the lives of the children and families she counseled. This inspired her to start her own journey of faith and personal growth through writing, digital creating, and public speaking. Her words have provided comfort, guidance, and inspiration to many, helping them deepen their relationship with God and navigate life's challenges with grace and resilience.

In addition to her writing, Jennifer is a successful entrepreneur and nonprofit leader. Her passion for helping others led her to found Gr8t•i•Am Mississippi Inc, a 501(c)(3) dedicated to supporting and empowering young people and families in need. Through her work in both the mental health and business worlds, Jennifer has become a respected leader and advocate for those in need, inspiring others to pursue their dreams and positively impact the world. Jennifer's life is a testament to the power of faith, resilience, and a deep commitment to serving others. Through her words and actions, she has demonstrated that anything is possible when we believe in ourselves, our God-given purpose, and, most importantly, God. Her story inspires all who seek to make a difference in the world, reminding us that we can overcome any obstacle and achieve our dreams with determination, faith, and love. The sky is the limit for this up-and-coming Author and all-around talent.

Follow her rise at JENNIFEROSHANNONMEDIA.COM
Scan this QR code to connect with Jennifer!

Abraham Experience
By Crystal Drayton

When I think of *God Tough*, many thoughts and testimonies come to mind. However, before sharing my personal testimony or experience, I believe it's important to share, what being God Tough means to me. I know it may be ironic, but when I think of God Tough, I think of times that I was most vulnerable. I think of times when I was at my weakest. I think of times when I had no more ideas, thoughts, or reasoning. I know you may believe this is the opposite of tough – please allow me to explain. During those experiences, this scripture comes to mind, 2 Corinthians 12:9 "My grace is sufficient for you, for my power is made perfect in weakness." I have a clear understanding, that his strength is made perfect in my weakest moments. When we are at our weakest, when we are at our lowest, when we are most vulnerable, that's when we can completely surrender and allow God to take control. It is at these moments that education, logic, reasoning, ideas, and experiences, don't matter because you're truly dependent on the

Father. The only way to truly experience being God Tough is when we allow his strength to rise up on the inside of us and to push through whatever we may be going though at that time. Now that I have clarified and defined what being God tough means to me, I would like to share one of my personal testimonies.

While I have many testimonies, there is a major one that comes to mind. It was the summer of 2021 when my husband called me. I could tell he was strong in his voice, but there was something that was bothering him. He proceeded to tell me that our current landlord was only giving us three to four months to either purchase the townhome we were in, or we would have to move out. Immediately, my heart dropped to my chest. As a mother of three children who were 7, 8, and 11 at the time, I started to worry about having a roof over my children's head. While my husband and I talked about purchasing a home in the future, we were not in a position to do so at that moment. I remained strong while I was on the phone with him; however, once the phone conversation ended, I immediately dropped to my knees and began to pray. There was an overwhelming number of thoughts and feelings that surrounded my heart and mind, and I knew the only way to achieve peace was to cast my cares on God.

When I finished praying, reality hit and all I could say is Father, I trust you. The home we were renting was a beautiful three-story, three-bedroom townhome in a gated community. The majority of our neighbors were retired and there weren't many children in the neighborhood. Inside of the home, there were two master bedrooms. We were in one master and our children were in the other. When we first moved in, our children were very small so sharing a room with bunk beds were doable. However, we knew our family was growing and eventually we would have to move, we just didn't think it would be so soon. We are a family that tries to apply faith with action in any area that we can. Before my husband received the news, we always had one box packed by the door because we believed God was going to put us in our own home one day. We just didn't know he would do it this way. God started to bring back to my remembrance the little warnings he was given us. For example, there were at least 3 different neighbors that connected with us on three different occasions and they all would say "hey are you guys moving". We would always respond with maybe sometime in the future, but not any time soon. This occurred at least 6 months prior to receiving the news. I would always tell my husband I wonder why they are asking us that.

God brought all those moments back to my remembrance. Furthermore, he reminded me that I would say in my time of prayer that I am the seed of Abraham and an heir according to the promise.

Holy Spirit whispered, "You want the promises connected to Abraham, but never considered his experience; this is your Abraham experience."

Holy Spirit was right, I wanted the promises connected to Abraham, but I never considered having to go through an Abraham experience where I would have to pack up my family and have no idea where we were going.

After having this conversation with the Lord, I changed my language and started to say, "This is my Abraham experience."

I can recall one morning after I prayed; the Lord lead me go on Facebook. As soon as I did, Apostle Yolanda was on live and encouraging everyone. Of course, I clicked to listen to try to take in any encouragement at that time. On her live, she saw that I was viewing, and she gave me a prophetic word. She called my name and said she saw a house, and she didn't know if my husband and I were looking to move or buy, but God showed her a house. She said that God was going to give us the house based on our faithfulness to ministry.

After she gave me this word, she begins to sing, this is the day, this is the day, that the Lord has made. You know the rest. The way she was singing was a slow peaceful melody and it hit my spirit in a way I just can't explain. Of course, the tears started to flow, and I could not wait to tell my husband what the Lord just spoke through his prophet. She had no idea what we were going through she lives in another state, goes to another ministry, and this truly came straight from the Father.

Receiving that word was such a relief. While our situation did not change, it just was a relief to know that God sees and not only does he see, but he made us aware of his plans.

God gave us a prophecy to hold on to, and we did just that. Every day that I drove to work I would listen to the same prophecy. Every time that I felt discouraged, I would listen to the prophecy and the song. Every time that we received bad news, I would listen to the prophecy. Every time that fear tried to arise, I would listen to the prophecy.

There are times we may not have the strength or encouragement within ourselves to get through the day. When I had my weakest moments, I listened to the prophecy over and over and over again. This was to remind myself and remind my spirit what the Lord had promised. This is what being God tough is all about! Allowing God to rein and direct your life even when you don't understand.

Over the course of time, we started packing boxes, and we told our children what we were believing God for. This was not only to make them aware of what was going on, but we wanted to strengthen their faith as well. One day my middle child came to us, Nevaeh and she said, "Mommy I had a dream that our house was surrounded by trees in the backyard." I immediately knew that was God showing her our home. This was unusual for our middle child, and I knew that the Lord was showing us once again what he had in store for us.

Please know those three to four months were difficult. I still cried, I still worried, fear tried to come in, but I did not allow those emotions to stay. I fought those emotions with prayer, listening to the prophecy, and speaking what the word says concerning our family. This was truly a walk by faith, not by sight experience. This was truly his strength is made perfect in our weakness experience. This was my Abraham experience. This was God tough!

During those months of moving and preparation, we believed that God would help us with our credit reports, get an approved lender, provide us enough for the down payment, and place us in the right home. We had to do this in a time when it did not make sense to purchase a home. The market was a sellers' market and not a buyers' market. Home prices were ridiculously expensive. Sellers were posting their available homes one day, and they would go under contract within a week. We had all odds against us, and nothing we were faced with made sense. However, we knew that what is impossible with man is possible with God (Luke 18:27). Through the tears, we believed; through the uncertainty, we believed; through the negative odds, we believed.

In those three to four months, our credit scores began to increase; we received several approvals from lenders, and we received unexpected funds to cover our down payment. God was blowing our minds left and right. With all of our financial affairs in order, we still had to find a home. After-all, they were going like hotcakes. I will never forget during my time of prayer; God told me to write down the number of rooms and bathrooms that I wanted. At that time, I'm going to be honest, I said God, the details don't matter; I just don't want to be homeless! What I love about the Father we serve is even in situations where we would settle for less, he brings back to our remembrance that we are royalty, we are heirs of the King, and he wants us to have the desires of our hearts within his will. I just wanted a home, but he reminded me that I could have the home I desired.

I wrote on a piece of paper five bedrooms, three bathrooms with a basement. I also wanted the kitchen to be open to the living room so when I'm cooking; I won't miss any family time. I put the paper in my prayer box and smiled.

The first house we went to see was beautiful, but it did not match the paper in my prayer box. However, I loved the home and decided to go for it. When it was time for the owner to accept the bids, the owner changed his mind and decided not to sell the house. My husband encouraged me and said "Babe, that's just not the one for us." We looked at several homes; none really matched what we needed for our family. I will never forget during my time of prayer, I said Father, please dispatch your angels to the land and home that you have for us and guide us to the promise. I didn't want to waste time and expectation on a home that wasn't meant for us. Shortly after we found a beautiful 5 bedroom, 4 bathrooms, with a completed basement house surrounded by trees in the backyard. This home not only matched the paper in my prayer box, my daughters dream, but it was beyond what we wanted. We knew this was the one.

I took pictures of the home, created a vision board with PowerPoint, and put Drayton Estate over the pictures. This home was different; this home was beyond our expectations.

Fast forward to the last day we were allowed in our townhome; we were cleaning and packing up boxes. My husband received a call while we were packing from our real-estate agent. When she called, everything went silent, and we stood still. She proceeded to say that the owner accepted our offer out of the 5 they received. All we could do was cry and thank God. God confirmed his promise to us. As you know, there are still aspects that must be completed after the offer is accepted, but I would need another chapter to share the small battles and small wins in between. However, I'm here today to tell you that God did it! We are now homeowners of 5 bedrooms, four bathrooms, and a completed basement home. Not only that, but we also pay less in mortgage than what we were paying to rent our townhome. This was truly God-ordained. The townhouse we were in was on Sailors Lane, the home that we purchased is on Anchors Way! God Anchored us in the home that he had for us.

I will never forget how we broke the news to our children. We told them we were going to dinner at a friend's house. When we pulled up, we said surprise this is our home. They could not believe it! They ran out of the car and started running around, and I can still hear the sound of my son's voice saying he did it, God did it, God did it! I get filled up now remembering that moment because not only were we believing God, so were our children. I know that a faith experience will stick with them into their adulthood. God did it, and I am a firm witness that God's promises are yes and amen! God gave me the strength and the ability to be God tough through the entire process. I had to be God tough for my husband, I had to be God tough for my children, and I had to be God tough for myself. The only way to really be God tough is to truly allow God's strength to rise up on the inside of you when you are at your weakest. It's when we allow him to lead and trust his direction and his promises. If you are ever in a situation when you have to completely rely on the Father to make a way, just remember that's the perfect opportunity to be God Tough.

CRYSTAL DRAYTON

rystal Drayton is a wife, mother, Youth Director, ordained Minister of the Gospel of Jesus Christ, and a creative entrepreneur. She is married to Robert Drayton, and together they have three beautiful children Amira, Nevaeh, and Ezekiel Drayton. Crystal is the founder of Crystal's Creations Events where she can apply her expertise she obtained as a Sales Event Manager at Hyatt Corporations. Crystal is also the founder of I Am Ministry where she enjoys uplifting and empowering individuals with the tools and strategies to see themselves through the eyes of God. She believes that all of us have something unique to offer the world and what better way to do this than to consult the creator. Most of all Crystal enjoys creating new memories with her family and spending time with her loved ones.

It Should Have Broken Me, But It Made Me Stronger

By Roniesha Fosque

The foundation of my entire life was always built on God. My mother made sure of that. She raised us in church and made sure our faith was built firm on being God Tough. That was my mom, though. She wasn't perfect; however, she stayed strong in her faith. And even though she and I didn't have much of a mother/daughter relationship, she did the best that she could to protect me. My dad, on the other hand, played a different part in my life. Actually, he didn't play a role in my life at all. I met my dad when I was 35 years old. That was after he served a 46-year sentence in prison.

As a little girl, I always dreamed of the perfect life—my mother and father in the household in love and raising me together. I held on to that dream for a long time. It was the one thing that got me through from day to day as a little girl. I didn't have that love flowing like in a normal family. The insecurities, low self-esteem, and lack of self-confidence consumed me as a child. I can remember walking with my head down and often feeling like the black sheep of the family. I'm sure it was very noticeable, especially to my mom's new boyfriend.

I remember the day that she met him. We were walking and saw him. He was very into my mom. I didn't like it. I knew it was something off about him. We later found out that he lied about his identity. He was not a Christian at all. Neither was he single. He was a Muslim, married, and had children. I didn't like this guy at all. Yes, because he lied about who he was, but more so because when my mom started dating him, we stopped visiting my dad. This really broke my heart. But I continued to hold on to my dream of them still getting back together. I remember one Sunday, my mom and I came home from church, and this man's wife was also at the house. I really believe this man had witchcraft on my mom.

Why else would she put up with this type of behavior? Why would she belittle herself to being with a man who has a wife and family and be comfortable with his wife in the same room? This whole thing was so weird to a 10-year-old. He even mentioned one time that he believed in the devil. That was scary to hear, knowing our foundation was God. That same day he looked me in my eyes and said, "Your mom and dad are not getting back together because she's with me." That crushed me.

I always wondered why his wife was there. And I questioned the role she played in this. One night, I was there with them alone. This was the scariest time of my life. I didn't understand what was happening or why it was happening to me. My mom's boyfriend held my hands down so tightly that I couldn't move. I just laid there as his wife molested me. Then they began to swap places and take turns. She would hold me down, and he would rape me. This happened on several occasions. He told me every time that he would kill me if I ever told anyone. I finally cried my last tear. I was tired of this happening to me. I needed to tell someone.

I finally found the strength to open up and tell my mom what was happening. But she didn't believe me. As a matter of fact, her exact words were, "Stop lying on him."

That shut me down completely. I was so hurt. I was mad and angry, and I felt so dirty. I was now 11 years old. I would constantly ask God, why? Why is this happening to me? Better yet, why does this keep happening to me? And now by different people. I started being molested by family members. And other men in my mom's life molested me as well. I remember two of them exactly. Everyone was touching on me so much that I began to think this was ok. They would even start to give me money, not to tell. I really thought this was a normal life. I became numb to it. Nobody believed me anyway. My own mom didn't. So, who else could I tell? Who else would believe me?

My mom would make me go over to my aunt's house sometimes. I don't know why, but I slipped and told her what was happening to me. And she actually believed me! I'll never forget when she showed up at that house with her cane, ready to fight for me! From that point on, I had a new love and respect for my aunt. I don't blame my mom for anything that happened to me. I knew she loved me. I knew she wanted to protect me. She was blinded by love. Or what she thought was love. Her type of love was witchcraft. It consumed her. And eventually, I think even she knew that it would be the death of her.

One night she made me go to my aunt's house. For the life of me, I did not want to go. I begged and cried for her just to let me stay with her. That night just seemed different. I had never cried so hard to stay with my mom. Through all of the tears, she still made me go. My mom had these green eyes. They were like mood-changing eyes that would leave anyone mesmerized. And when I looked into her eyes that night, I knew something was off. She knew something that she wasn't telling me. It was very dark that night. Darker than a normal night. I was finally at my aunt's house resting.

Hours later, the next-door neighbor came banging on the door and said that they just took my mom to the hospital. As soon as I heard that, I said to myself, "My mom is gone."

We rushed to the hospital. When we walked in, he was there. Her boyfriend with the wife that had been molesting me. He looked like a demon. His eyes were so glassy and scary. Rage came over me, and I yelled, "You killed my mom!" I kept yelling it over and over as loud as I could. He just looked at me. He didn't say anything. And I kept yelling it. He looked so evil. My mom was gone.

The doctors finally let us back to see her. I broke down. She was naked. She had foam coming from her mouth, and dirt was in her hair like she had been dragged through the grass. I began to scream again, "You killed my mom!" Again. They didn't believe me. People kept saying it was her time to go, but they also didn't know what I knew. The doctor said that she had a massive heart attack. I knew that wasn't true. He lied to the hospital and told them that they were married and, due to their religion, they did not want an autopsy done.

The day of my mom's funeral was one of the hardest things that I had to deal with. My family had to take me to the casket. I didn't want to see her like that. I cried, but I never really mourned. I was just so angry. I knew that this man murdered my mom, and he was going to get away with it. After the funeral, he, his wife, and his kids fled the state in the middle of the night. And no one could find him after that. He even took the lockbox with him that had all of my moms and me and my sibling's personal information in it. I would have dreams about him often. I always wondered what I would do if I ever saw him again.

One day, in my adulthood, I found the strength to search for him and his family. I found his daughter on social media and reached out. I was surprised that she remembered me. She told me that her mom (the wife) had passed away. And that he was still alive. He was now in jail, serving a life sentence. At that moment, I understood the meaning of two things, "God has the final say, and Vengeance is the Lord's."

He may have gotten away with murdering my mom, but something caught up with him. My prayer is that while he is in there, he can find healing for his mind. And forgiveness for everything that he has done. After deeper conversations with his daughter, I later discovered he had also molested her. He really had some deep mental and sick issues. Prayerfully that was God's way of getting him out of the normal population so that he couldn't hurt anyone else.

After my mom passed, my aunt raised me from that point until adulthood. And it started again. The molestation. This time from family members again. I told my aunt because she was the only one who believed me the last time. This time she didn't. No one did.

Being molested and introduced to sex at such an early age really opened up windows. I just wanted someone to love me. I was looking for love in all the wrong places. I was so desperate for love that I even entertained dating females. I just wanted love. It didn't matter where it came from. I started dating drug dealers and men that were very mean to me. I finally got tired of being in these relationships that were going nowhere. And there was no love.

I said, "Lord, I'm ready to settle down."

But I believe the devil heard me too and sent me a counterfeit. I allowed this man in my life that would physically abuse me. He would always call me ugly (with a few choice words after that). This damaged what little self-esteem I had left. I finally decided that I needed a backbone and that I had to learn to stand up for myself. I was tired of the abuse. I had been mentally, physically, and emotionally abused since I was a little girl. And it was time for it to STOP! God sent this beautiful, spirited woman into my life. I adopted her as my spiritual mother. She really brought me out of my shell. She taught me to smile and to walk with my head up. She gave me that motherly nurturing that I needed. I found my backbone.

Whenever my boyfriend would hit me, I would never fight back. I was still that scared little girl inside, I guess. But one day, he raised his hand to hit me, and I got right in his face. I finally stood up to him! And he backed up. He never hit me again! At that moment, I learned that sometimes people just need to know that you aren't scared of them. Fear attracts bad people to do bad things. It took a while, but now I know that God didn't give me the spirit of fear but of love, peace, and a sound mind.

I had to learn about life on my own. I learned through life experiences. I would fall and get back up. Falling and getting back up was on repeat for a long time. The battles with low self-esteem and thoughts of suicide consumed me many of nights. I was tired of men leaving me after sex. I was tired of giving my body away and sometimes for money to make it. I was tired of addictions to numb pain. I was just tired. I had many heartbreaks, scars, and bruises. I realize that this journey should have broken me. However, it's made me stronger. Now I am free from it all! Everything that the devil through at me I broke free from. This journey has taught me how to forgive, how to love myself and others, and patience. I thank God so much for my journey. It's taught me that God will never leave me and that there is more in me than what stood against me. It's taught me that I'm Built God Tough.

Roniesha Fosque

Roniesha Fosque grew up in Maryland and has also worked in the medical field as a GNA/Medical Assistant since "2003". She has her own uniform business called "Blessed by the Best Scrubs," which she invested in "2021". Her Faith is powerfully built on the scripture that she lives by "I can do all things through Christ who strengthens me." She's a very honest person known for her passionate spirit and for giving back to her community, making a difference in people's lives. Roniesha had only three pregnancies and five children. She enjoys spending time with them and setting a good foundation for each of them. She loves cooking, surrounding herself with positive people, and being a blessing to others.

E-mail: RonieshaFosque@yahoo.com
Facebook: Blessed by the Best Scrubs
Facebook: Roniesha Fosque

Dust Yourself Off
And Try Again
By Brandi Nichole Wallace

Our greatest weakness lies in giving up. The surest way to succeed is always to try just one more time. -- Thomas A. Edison

Today, I present to you a successful woman in the marketplace. However, it has not always been this way, nor have I had the confidence to say I was successful in any business area. Becoming who I envisioned myself as an entrepreneur always seems far-fetched because of life-changing circumstances. Primarily dealing with a situation where it looks like your dream has finally come true, but in less than a year, the dream has become a nightmare. Then, when I finally thought I had it together in one area, another area showed up with unexpected situations that would cause doubt and fear. But the key is never to give up. No matter how often you have to start over, move forward. But giving up is never an option. While I have been an entrepreneur since I was 18 years old, there were times when I thought I was gaining ground in my pursuit but ended up hitting dead ends. Desiring to make six figures, only to see six figures in the negative within the first two years of starting my first business.

When it comes to entrepreneurship, it is definitely not for the weak. Pursuing entrepreneurship takes discipline, tenacity, focus, persistence, and wisdom. It is definitely a calling, and one must be graced in business. And that was me because I could never stay on a job for longer than a year or two. But working for myself seemed to last longer than two years. It was a consistent pattern, and the writing on the wall was apparent that I was called to entrepreneurship.

So, what about my journey in business made me who I am today? In 2008, my 1st business was Studio 77 Hair Salon in Owings Mills, MD. I had an investor whom I'd met through my previous salon employer, so we met in person to discuss business and talk numbers. ** I felt like a REAL BOSS. ** After hearing my vision, the investor agreed to invest $20,000 but I would only need to pay back 50% if I allowed him to become a partner, but only for three years. Does this sound like a yellow flag? So, once we agreed verbally, contracts had to be done.

A few days later, the investor and I met up to deposit the money and sign the contract. Exciting, right? No, he handed me two contracts on neon green and pink paper, $20,000 CASH, but could only deposit $9999 in a bank account at a time, IMMEDIATELY I was feeling nervous, but because this was my first salon, I wanted to pursue it. I naturally knew that he should have given me a cashier's check but out of ambition and excitement, I settled for the cash, no paper trail. So, moving forward, the salon is in the whole operation, and the investor came to the salon as if he owned it and started to try to take the money from the cash register. The situation was so bad that I had placed a restraining order on him. Later a stylist applied to become a booth renter and was hired. She worked for me for a month until one morning, I received a phone call from an employee that I needed to get to the salon asap. When I arrived, everything in my salon was gone. The stylist was sent to set me up, and from that moment, I felt like someone had raped me of my dreams. It was this moment that I never wanted to do business again; it was this moment that paralyzed me in moving into my next; it was this moment that had me stagnant; every negative emotion that you could possibly think of, I had it. From anger to fear, doubt, DEFEAT.

So, how did I get through it? The answer was "Go through the grieving process." We must understand that whenever we go through a moment of loss in any capacity, we must grieve the loss. I took a few months off while in the process of still having to rebuild my salon. And so, once I reopened after the loss. Unfortunately, it was never the same, and I ended up fully closing my salon, which has me in debt of $189,000, filing for Chapter 7 bankruptcy at the age of 26.

Once again, another added emotion of guilt, disappointment, and DEFEAT. At this point, I had hit rock bottom and wasn't sure if I wanted to get it. Usually, you will feel like you couldn't, but I didn't want to. I am 26 years old and have now experienced a failed business while going through a divorce at the same time. Yeah, I'm not getting up from this. Again, grieving the loss of a company, marriage, and finances. You may ask, what did I do next? I eventually got a job at a chain salon and started over with my life. But it was never in the capacity of how the Lord wanted me to function. I had settled in working for someone else business because I was afraid to launch back out. It was during this season that Romans 8:28 became so real to me. "And we know that all things work together for the good of those who love the Lord and are called according to His purpose.

Although fearful, God used every business experience after my loss to build me back up. In each situation after that, God would have me in the set for a year, then I would move on to the next. In that recovery season, I was able to birth another business but still fearful of opening a brick-and-mortar. I played it safe, but God was still building me, and this went on for at least nine years. Then, one day was November 4th, 2021, in the 10th year. He said clearly, "GO, look for your building." That was when I knew I had to be obedient because WHATEVER He had planned, I needed to execute ASAP. So, I went. Today, I present a successful businesswoman in the marketplace who has also embraced her call-in ministry in the totality of who God called and positioned me. I had to dust myself off many times and try again. With fear in my heart, I toiled.

Who do I trust? But with a mindset, I am still moving forward. And in every situation, layers were falling and being re-established simultaneously. The most significant setback has set me up for the greatest comeback.

BRANDI NICHOLE WALLACE

Brandi **Nichole Wallace** is an International Award-Winning Stylist, Confidence Coach, Beauty Educator, Author, Speaker, and Marketplace Prophet. She recently received her certification as a Hair Loss Practitioner, Trichologist, and Nutrition Consultant as a Drugless Practitioner. She also has earned a Master's Degree in Professional

Cosmetology. As the owner of The Hair Clinic Rx, she has evolved into the hair restoration industry, allowing her to assist clients with hair loss concerns and build their confidence.

Brandi Nichole Wallace has been involved with local, national, and international opportunities doing photo shoots for production companies and various photographers in the United Kingdom, DC-Maryland-Virginia (D.M.V.), Atlanta Metropolitan area, New Jersey, New York, NY and Houston, Tx. She was also a contributing writer for B.N.B. magazine in Japan, sharing her knowledge and expertise about the hair care industry with over 7,500 subscribers internationally. Her latest accomplishment was being one of the hairstylists in Essence Magazine for Black Women of the White House and being the 1st Celebrity Stylist to make the cover internationally for OKHair Magazine, launched in Brazil. She won her first award as Best Hair Stylist in Houston, TX, in 2016 and has been a 3x Nominee for the Fashion Awards. Her celebrity clients include Porsha Williams from Housewives of Atlanta, Music Group Shop Boyz, and Melessa Denee, hairstylist of The Braxton's, to name a few.

She has over 21 years of experience as a licensed Senior and Master Cosmetologist, Makeup Artist, and Image Consultant, making her a triple threat. And with15 years of Beauty Education, her passion and purpose are to uplift and build positive self-esteem through appearance transformation, behavior development, communication, and creating a digital footprint image. She understands the benefits of continuing education and strives to remain current by continuously enhancing her skills and techniques and educating others to build their image and confidence through personal image branding.

Brandi Nichole Wallace also provides hair care and confidence coaching. She loves to inspire and encourage women through her empowerment to Bee C.H.I.C: Confident, Healed, Interdependent, and Courageous. Her life's vision is to show women the importance of maintaining their confidence within themselves and pursuing courage so that healthy business and personal relationships are established in their lives.

Website: iambrandinichole.com
email: info@iambrandinichole.com

He Had His Hands On Me

Growing Pains

By Carolyn Harris

The question was, why did you say yes to being an author in the Built God Tough Anthology? My answer was because that's who I am, Built God Tough. The enemy tried to take me out and kill the seed God had planted. The enemy thought that the molestation and rape would break me and cause me to give up, but "he had his hands on me."

After the rape, it did leave me feeling damaged and broken, But God! As a little girl, I always said that I didn't want to go through what my mother went through. All she wanted was to be loved. My mom was a beautiful woman inside and out. She wanted to be that homemaker and the foundation for her family, and she was so much more than that.

As we get older, we do learn of our worth. Back to my story, my mom found herself attracted to one of my brother's friends. She did move him into our home. I will never understand why she felt the need to do that because she was doing fine by herself, but I get it, we as women think we need a man to complete us. Now I know better. All I needed was for God to come and live inside me.

I am the baby out of six. I have three brothers and two sisters, one brother by another mother and a sister by another mother. All of my other siblings in the same household had the same father. The enemy tried to make me feel like I didn't fit in, but I knew that was a lie because I was so spoiled by both sides of my family. Back to the story, after maybe a year of my brother's friend living with us, I found myself being left with him a lot because my mom was working a lot, and my siblings were older, so they were always out doing their own thing. I felt in my spirit that this guy was not right for my mom. Well anyway he ended up molesting me. I told my mom, and she didn't believe me. Her words were "why would he do that when he has me." That hurt me to heart. You hear stories about mothers that do end up putting their men before their children. In God's word, he said he will provide a way out. As I sit and think about it now, there was a time when my aunt and uncle on my dad's side had asked my mom if she wanted them to help raise me, and they were well off, but they couldn't have any kids. Mom asked me how I would feel about that.

I said that I couldn't imagine being without my mom and no way. Now was that my way of escape from what the enemy had planted for me. That did not work! The molestation continued for a couple of years to the point where if I wanted to hang out with my friends, I had to let him touch me; no one had a clue what I had to endure just to have a childhood. He had his hands on me. When I think back, he groomed me, which means the practice of preparing or training someone for a particular purpose or activity. My mom ended up catching him in the act, and it broke her heart. It hurt me to heart to see her that way when all she wanted was to love and be loved I ended up having issues with trusting people, even my mom. I truly felt like how I could you allow this to happen to me, but now I know God allows us to go through things that we think are going to break us, but he already knows that we are built God tough. I just love him. My God has been so good to me; yes, I have been through a lot. It didn't break me, it didn't take me out, it made me into the woman I am today. I am so glad "He had his hands on me." Now, this is not how the story ends, so you will have to look out for the next book because there is so much more I have to give God the glory for, but when God said in his word in Romans 8:18 "I consider that the suffering of this present time is not worth comparing with the glory that is to be revealed to us. "

Oh boy, and in his word in Haggai 2:9," the glory of this latter temple shall be greater than the former says the lord of hosts, and in this place, I will give peace says the lord of host ", all I can say is my God, my God. Be blessed. Love you with the love of God.

CAROLYN JUANITA HARRIS

Carolyn Juanita Harris is a God-fearing woman who has a passion for God's word and women's ministry and marriage ministry she is the wife to Kevin I Harris she is a mother and a grandmother and a sister, an aunt, and a sister in Christ to many. She is a teacher assistant she has been a caregiver most of her life she has a few certifications under her belt. She is a member of Abrams Memorial Church, where Thomas

Fisher is the pastor and Vivian Fisher is the first lady. Carolyn is on the Praise team and loves to praise the lord everywhere she goes. Matthew 22: 14 states that for many are called, but few are chosen; she has chosen to be a vessel for the lord and has been committed to letting the whole world know. Her favorite scripture is Matthew 11: 28 come to me, I will give you rest. And Philippians 4: 13   I can do all things through   Christ.

My email: harris668carolyn@outlook.com

My website: www. staytruecarolynjharris.com

I Made It!

By Landes Hubbard

My story, my testimony, my healing, and my breakthrough. I pray this may help anyone going through taking care of a loved one. Hold on; God will surely take care of you.

My mother was the most loving and caring person you would ever want to meet. Over the years of my growing up as a child, to a teenager, to an adult I watched my mother take care of all of us that were in our household. She made sure that we all had breakfast and hot meals when we came home from school. She always made sure we had just what we needed. My mother was a God-fearing woman that loved the Lord, and we all went to church every Sunday morning. Even when me and my sister went out clubbing and didn't want to get up, she would always tell us you went out last night, so you're going to church this morning. Sometimes I was so hung over. I had to get myself right for Sunday afternoon service as well. My mom didn't play that. I wasn't saved then, but she said as for this household, you will go to church.

My mom made sure we were always together every holiday. That's Easter, Mother's Day, Father's Day, birthdays, Christmas, and Thanksgiving. My mom was something else! Her nickname was "Bitty" because she was so tiny and very soft-spoken with a unique voice, but trust me, when she said something and meant it, we all knew she meant business. She was the chain that always kept all of us connected and together.

I had previous jobs along the way. I worked at ConAgra, Black & Decker, and then I got laid off, and then I just helped my mom take care of my dad with the help of my sister. I watched my mom take care of my dad and all of us at the same time, again making sure he and we had all that we needed as always. This woman was a strong, black little woman. The passing of my dad in 1994 fell on our mother hard. She was a loving and caring wife to my dad until his passing. Here was this woman handling a household now all alone. And what little I could do to help, I did. We both worked out things together. I did what I could, but my mom took most of it. Again, this was a strong woman; I just can't express enough how strong she was. And how God-loving she was. She really loved the Lord with all of her heart and was a great example to all of us.

I watched her go through all of this with an illness of her own starting to creep in a little at a time. She loved to go to church, so my sister and I would see to it that she made it there even as she took ill. My niece would take her to church as well. She always loved to dress up, and she could dress! She was always in church until her health would not allow her to go anymore. She had written a paper that started like this, "I started this walk with God years ago when I was young at Queen Esther, AME church in Ivory town...."

She sang in the church choir, and if you knew my mom, she was a mockingbird. She could *sang*! She gave a lot of church recitals. She just loved to sing. She later formed a family group called the Silvertones, the gospel singers; my brother played the guitar for them. And more family members sang with her as well. She also sang with the Maryland Harmonetts and the Preston Circuit Choir.

Much time passed on, and many changes took place in her life. Now, she couldn't see as well, and she didn't walk as swiftly anymore, but she wrote to the church again, "I'm blessed..." She said she was under the doctor's care, but she also said, "I have a doctor that is above all doctors, and his name is Jesus, and He is my primary doctor..." as she resigned from the choir, she said she would continue to sing in her seat, even though her breathing may get short, sometimes, and if, and when the time comes that she cannot say a word, or sing a note, "I will just wave my hand and give God glory as all honor and glory belongs to him" she said. "Please pray my strength in the Lord and that I will forever do his will," she continued to write.

My whole world changed at that moment. I can't remember the specific dates that we had to take my mom back and forth to the doctor's office and hospital. Some things just started to happen so quickly to my mom's health that I don't recall each day. My brother said mom had some acting-out ways that my aunt would sometimes have before she passed. My mom would act out like she wasn't feeling good, and sometimes this would happen when me and my sister said we were going out.

We did take her to the hospital many times, but they couldn't find anything wrong with her, so this continued to happen for a while; then, over the past times later on, she would just act out and not remember anything. Then she lost her hearing. Sometimes her ears would stay clogged up, and when we went to the doctor's appointment with her, me, my sister, my brother, and sister-in-law, when she couldn't hear, she would just read lips. She didn't like the fact that she couldn't hear, then when the doctor gave his diagnosis, I began to secret cry. From that time on, she wouldn't know you sometimes. I remember we had a family meeting at the house, and she said to them, "Who is that girl sitting at the dining room table?" it was me, but she didn't know who I was.

She would start to say at night, when she went to bed, someone was after her and someone was pouring water down her back, and then it became real. My mom had dementia. We were in and out of the doctor's offices and hospitals all the time. She would always think and say that either my son or my nephew was messing with her feet; I would look and say, "Mom, no one is messing with your feet."

She would get mad, and I would ask her. "Do you want to go to a nursing home?" she would yell, "NO!" And calm right down. That's something I would've never done, but if I said that, she would calm down. When family would come and see her, she would repeat herself over and over and then do it more often. I remember we were preparing to get something done to the house, and my mom just went off and said, "Why are you here?"

At that time, I was ready to leave. I was done. My sister picked me up and took me across the bridge; I told my sister I wasn't going back. She then proceeded to call my brother, and they talked. Then my sister talked to me, and I eventually went back. I would just stay in my room. I still did what needed to be done for my mother, though. I bathed her and made sure her hair was done and made sure she ate. It was very stressful, but I did what needed to be done for my mother.

She loved to eat. I gave her a bell for if I was still sleeping, so she could just ring the bell if she got hungry. Big mistake. That bell was constantly ringing all the time. Every time family members would come over, she would be happy and nice, but then when it was just me and her, she acted like she didn't want me there. I talked to my sister about it when my sister would come and take her to the family dollar store.

My mother loved that store. My sister said to me, "Landes, mom said she likes when I take her to the store because I let her look around, but you just want her to hurry up," but she would be in there forever. I had to eventually take a leave of absence because I said I would never put my mother in a nursing home! So, when my sister would take me out just to get me out of the house, we had family friends that would come and stay with her until we got back. We would sit in the restaurant eating, and the phone would ring; I already knew it was my mom, and she wanted us to return. I didn't get to go out anywhere. I had to constantly stay in that house with my mom. I had no life. It was just taking care of my mom. My sister thought that I would pass away before my mom. I was just so stressed, and it was so hard on me taking care of a household and my mother. This went on daily, and as I said still in and out of hospitals.

I remember when my cousin passed away. He lived next door, and that was my mom's boy. I remember seeing my mom so in an uproar that she ran over to his house next door and then ran back to our house; I don't even think she knew what she was doing, but it took a lot out of her. And she had to be rushed to the hospital that same night. She was on a ventilator for days. I got a phone call from the hospital because I had just had surgery a week prior to this, my sister-in-law handed me the phone, and I let her listen. She said the hospital wanted to know if my mom had to be resuscitated would she want to be? I fell right down to the floor, crying. My sister-in-law talked to me, and I said, "Me and my mom had never talked about that," so when she got out of the hospital, we did, and we got everything taken care of. She made it through that moment, even after all the running. However, her health steadily decreased over time.

As time went on, my mother passed away on November 25, 2010. My whole world just crashed. With each day that went on, it got harder to stay in that house that we shared together. I would close the mini blinds that led into her room because I would see her face. I had to take all of her pictures off of the wall so that I could get myself together. I would find myself sitting on the stool in the kitchen, just crying. Finally, my sister told me to pack myself and some clothes and come to her house, so I did that. I would stay there at night and then go home in the morning. I missed my mom so much. She would always be there when I got off of work, so it was different going home to her not being there. All of the lights in the house would always be on, and I would be one foot behind my mother. That's just how it always was. I would just sit remembering the good times we shared in that house before she got really down.

I would continue to go over to my sisters at night. I did this for four months. One morning I was coming down the stairs, and I fell. I sat on that step, and I cried. She asked me why I was crying. Was it because you fell or because you wanted to go home? I replied I want to go home. At that time, I did go home. I got home, and I just prayed that God would give me the strength to stay there by myself and to go through this process so that I could learn how to live at my house by myself. I got myself together and started going to church. I'm telling you; I don't know how in the world I would have made it if it hadn't been for my Lord and Savior, Jesus Christ. I thought I was going to die because all I wanted was to be with my mom. As I grew deeper into the Lord, he heard my cries, and I grew closer to Him. It was a struggle maintaining the whole household, but I did it. My family was always there for me to catch my back, but God did just what he said he would do. He showed up for me when I thought I couldn't make it without my mom. Just know that there is nothing too hard for my God. And if he brought me out, he could surely do the same for you. Have faith, be patient, be still, and wait on God. The devil thought he had me, but my God had me all along. God saved my life! I made it. My soul has been anchored in the Lord. God is good y'all. I am a winner!

Mold and guide me to your purpose, Lord, because I trust that your plans are better than I could ever ask for. God created us to love one another and to love our enemies. Also, through it all, John 3:16 says, for God so loved the world that he gave his only begotten son, that whoever believes in him shall not perish, but shall have eternal life. Be still and wait on God!

LANDES HUBBARD

I am a loving, caring, and devoted person. I will do anything I can to help family members. I can truly listen and give great wisdom and advice. I love the Lord with all of my heart. I am a mother in my ministry and genuinely love to help my ministry in any way I can. I have lots of faith and believe that God created me for a purpose.

So, I Thought I Was Crushed For The Crown. –What Makes Me God Tough By Mia Foster

I was never the popular pick, the one people always flocked to. But I carry something unique and sacred. Have you ever had a song that grows on you or a trend you pick up on later? Yup, that's me. I believe I can identify with those songs or trends because I've always been counted out, waiting for someone to recognize my value. They got a special tagline for those types; we call them the underdogs in the fight. Take special notice that others may see me as the underdog, but thanks to God, I'm no longer counting myself out. I'm choosing to see myself as the first-round draft pick in whatever scenario I find myself in. Of course, I didn't always see myself that way. I struggled with low self-esteem, low self-worth, and comparison syndrome. You know, the syndrome that keeps you looking around at everyone else's life, achievements, talents, and overall lifestyle? I understand that these struggles came as the norm of my worldly identity, but what happens when you get saved and become the daughter of The King, and you still must battle all of these stigmas in Christ?

I asked myself countless times, "Why do I have to go through this?" My "this" was my "yes" to God. I had enlisted in the army of the Lord; unbeknownst to me, I was really signing up for a crushing. This crushing came in the form of rejection of development. I went through plenty of seasons where all I wanted was a friend who was genuinely for me and reciprocated the love and loyalty I dished out. Instead, I was crushed by sisters who either didn't exemplify sisterhood, weren't walking the same path, or flat-out just didn't want to connect with me. But are you ready for this? It was all of God's plan. I received a prophetic word, where God let me know, it was Him. He was hiding me from people who would only damage me. Now I should've been ecstatic. At that moment, I cried out because I was moved that God loved me so much, He would go to such lengths to protect me. Oh, but when I got back by myself, I was shattered. I remember thinking about how long I really had to walk alone.

It took me some time to face the thoughts, feelings, and emotions connected to knowing I would have to build a deeper relationship with God by myself. Nobody else, no titles or talents to hide behind, just me and Him. I'd have to get to know Him alone. I'd have to unlearn the old version of me to accept my God-given identity in Christ. This even meant leaving some seasonal people behind. It took me being crushed by people to accept God's training methods. Sometimes it came in the form of canceled hangouts. Other times it was a lack of support. The most devastating was to be amongst the ones who just didn't get me or my purpose. How could they when I still had to learn it for myself?

I can admit that part of my disappointment stemmed from unrealistic expectations of others. What do I mean? Sometimes I expected others to show up in the situation how I would rather than accepting what they were showing me about them and their character. I had to depend on God to teach me who I am, what I'm worth, and the treatment I deserve. Of course, I kept trying to bring others into the mix until He confronted me and told me we were going to do things His way. He became commander and chief of my life. His way required letting go of pity parties and accepting accountability to guard my heart. Has it been easy of course not, but who can stand toe to toe with the Almighty? Submission is not easy, but necessary.

Eventually, I got in compliance. God began to show me that getting close to Him meant leaving the people who could harm God's plan and purpose for my life. I began to learn who I am and the strength that resides on the inside of me. I understand that my power comes from God, not people. I learned that I must learn to stand on my own, depending on God, before I invite anyone else into the fight. You might be saying, "Well, how did you cope?"

I'm glad you asked. There was no one size fits all remedy. Sometimes, I had to cry it out, literally sit in my feelings, pray, or read my bible. Other times I had no words and let my mind do the talking. In those moments, it took God's presence and peace. It took God's reassurance. It took Him rerouting my thoughts and shifting my outlook on self and the world around me. Christ literally took my crushing, allowing me to share my victory with you. I pray my story allows you to overcome your crushing experiences, knowing it is Jesus Christ who gets us through.

MIA FOSTER

M**ia Foster** is a #1 international bestseller of two anthologies, "Purpose in My Pain" and "I Am Stronger Than the Storm." She recently contributed to another women's faith-based devotional, "I Made It to the Other Side of Through." Mia has written countless poems and has a passion for reciting spoken word. She has released spoken word throughout social media, for her local assembly, and at women's empowerment events. Her captivating wordplay has captured the hearts of many as she explores topics centered around God, womanhood, and introspection. Mia is also an aspiring lyricist who enjoys writing the words to songs for other artists. As a domestic abuse survivor, Mia loves to encourage other women to be themselves to build self-esteem and is currently building an empowerment network for women, especially those who have survived domestic and sexual abuse.

Mia is an Eastern Shore, Maryland native. She is the mother of two beautiful girls. She loves family time, baking, learning, and all facets of art, especially creative writing, film, and music. She is currently pursuing a bachelor's degree in communication. As a creative, she hopes to continually answer her call of ministering to broken and battered women in authentic ways as God matures her in her walk with Jesus Christ.

DIE TO LIVE
BY JEANNE ELLIOTT

As a little girl, I would see visions of things; no matter what I was doing, they would come in little flashes of information, and just knowing of different things would be just unexplainable. I was scared to share my experiences. I kept them to myself, and then when I grew up with my own children, I would share certain things that I'd seen or felt. I had gotten to a point where my children didn't want me to say things because it would happen. My visions or dreams would be a little off but still correct.

September 20, 2020, I went to a funeral to support my friend whose coworker had suddenly passed away. At the funeral, the deceased son's mother grieved; something made me feel like I would be in that same place grieving on that front pew as they consoled her—that feeling consuming me.

I said "no" to myself, and I started thinking of each one of my three children, and I said "God, no!" Two weeks after this experience, I was in the bathroom, and here comes a vision of my son being hurt badly. He was lying on his back on the ground with his hands on his chest. I was trying to figure out the vision. Did someone try to rob him? Then my following vision was I needed to know my son's insurance information for the hospital. I got up and started praying and praying;

I found myself just staring at my son; all the time; I can remember just watching him sleep as I looked through the living room camera. I wanted to make sure he was breathing. I tried to erase that vision from me.

On October 23, 2020, when I went to my uncle's funeral. As my aunt went up to the casket for the final viewing, that feeling was back again; I remember my aunt shaking her head from side to side, crying. I had a vision. That was of me, standing in her place, shaking my head with tears. I was like, "No, God, no!"

Later that same night, I was awakened by a phone call from my daughter in a calm voice. I could tell she didn't want to get me upset. My son had been stabbed, and they called for an ambulance. The knowing feeling took over me as I could feel this wasn't good at all. When I got to the scene, the ambulance was driving off to the hospital. They didn't let me see or talk to my son; they only said, "The doctors are working on him, and they will call me with updates."

They only called me for insurance information. One of the police officers said that my son was talking and responding back. He thought he would be OK, but the knowing within me was telling me differently. I called my pastor at the time and one of my aunts for prayer. My children, friend, and I stayed in the parking lot for a little over three hours. My nerves were getting the best of me. My other two children were staying positive. My friend had to keep driving me home to use the bathroom. I could hear them talking and laughing at one another. As I was sitting in my friend's car, he was trying to encourage me that my son would be ok.

As he fell asleep on the driver's side, I couldn't stop crying. I prayed, and I cried. I prayed, and I cried.

I kept hearing an inner voice say, "You've got to choose, Bennie Smith's or Henry's Funeral Home?" I kept shaking my head, saying "no," and crying.

I knew my baby boy wasn't going to make it through this one. Once they called us in, I already knew. Then they put us in a small room, and the doctor talked. I was hoping he wouldn't say what I felt, but once he did, all I could say was, "I already knew."

October 24, 2020, at about 3 a.m. I took the hardest walk, and that was to see my baby boy, my son's lifeless body. As I walked closer, I saw my son's body. His head was to the side; my eyes went from his head down. I went back up to his face and looked at his beautiful eyebrows. Then I looked at the tattoo on his arm, and I broke down in tears. I felt my legs buckle. I had to get escorted out nothing left to do but to go back home to an empty home where I had raised him for 22 years. I was determined I wasn't going in there without him. I died with my son that morning. That Jeanne that everyone once knew would never be again.

The guilt started around 7 a.m. You're his mother, and you just left him there. You didn't even make it to his bedside. When I had the vision, did I not pray enough? Should I have warned him? Should I have told someone else my vision so they could have prayed with me. I was not there to protect him. God, with my depression, suicide attempts, and illness in my body, why would you let me live and take my son? At that time, I felt like my son's killer, and God stabbed me in my heart as well. Only mine was worse because they let me live that day. All I could do was cry. Everyone in my family that could come came that day. Even with them there, all I felt was my loss.

After a week of constantly weeping, my mood switched. I went into fight mode. My son's killer was on the run. I had to make sure he would be captured. At my son's funeral, my body was present, but I wasn't fully there. I suppressed my feelings, and my energy went on finding his killer; my cries to the Lord changed; I cried out for strength and guidance. I needed to see justice to the end. And whatever visions I'd seen, I fulfilled. I saw to get one with God, my children, my mother, and a few others.

Justice walks, community events, Facebook posts, different meetings, putting the killer's face on the news and in the newspapers, personally going to different towns, hanging flyers with his face on them, and constantly calling the chief of police and the states attorneys, I was determined to find justice for my son. Some people were saying I was doing too much. The nerve of them. If I could've done more, I would have. I never thought that I would be hated or disliked for fighting for justice for my son.

I literally had one of my son's family members unfriend me on social media and give her opinion about what I was doing. Yes, I was a little hurt but angrier. Then when a close family member made me feel like she hated me for this as well, I wasn't mad or angry, just totally devastated at this point. When it was told to me what she said... I was broken-hearted. But I couldn't give up the fight. I could not let that stop me. Even though, at times, I felt like I could lose my mind. Many times, I asked God where my support system was. I kept many things inside because I had no one to talk to, and if I did, who could I trust? How can I be so hated at a time like this? How can you judge me when you have never given birth to a child, or you have never lost a child to murder? How can you judge me? Even if you have experienced the death or murder of a child, you're fight of grief may not be the same as mine. My question to God was, how many times do I have to die in this process?

After I closed that casket on my son, I was fighting. And for those 17 months, I went through so many emotions. I needed to hear the prayers from my church, family, mothers, and other churches. I'm not going to say that they didn't pray. But I needed to hear the prayers; I needed to feel the love and support; I needed to hear it. I truly felt dropped by so many. I didn't get where people would bring you food to your home so you could grieve and have you rest so you didn't have to cook, but it was one person that God laid on her heart to buy me food from a restaurant twice. I got it, then. I never had any more to keep me company some days. I was left home alone. My one friend at the time would call to see if I was ok, if anyone stopped by call or text. My answer would always be no besides my children.

One of my cousins stopped by to check on me. I was so surprised. She said you're in this house alone.

I replied, "yes." That day I was a little overwhelmed. I was trying to find a church to have his funeral. I felt alone, but I wasn't. I was looking for people I thought, without a doubt, would show love and support me. God sent me certain people to encourage me that I would never think of; every time my energy got low, it might've been a stranger, my son's friends, or people I barely knew that would encourage me or send a gift. Many reached out to me through social media.

I had to realize I had to stop focusing on who wasn't there and focus on who was. I had an encounter in my front yard. It was a lady going past my home, and I was outside. She came back and said God told me to come back and pray with you. She asked me "May I pray with you." I said yes. that young lady prayed, and with every word she had spoken, I knew it was from God. God never left me, and, at that moment, I realized that it was a purpose for me to be isolated.

I started really focusing on my son at that point and our bond in his life. God blessed me with my son for 26 years. In those years, he often reminded me of my strength and my beauty. Yes, he thought his mom was beautiful, even at times when I didn't. He would say I was the strongest woman he knew, and I was his motivator. He even wrote these words in a song he did for me. So many people shared stories and testimonies of how my son helped encourage and show them love along this journey that we call life; my son shined his light on so many, and every one of those things helped me to live.

I didn't realize it was going to be another traumatizing experience, though. After two years, the murder trial was here, and after four days, the 12 jurors came back with a verdict of not guilty of murder but guilty of second-degree assault. I was traumatized. I couldn't say a word. The state's attorney was apologizing. They were shocked. A couple of tears fell down my face. I wouldn't allow anymore to flow. I walked out of that courthouse with my head held high.

Once I got to my vehicle, I broke down. I couldn't even drive. I wanted to hear a prayer but no calls, no texts, or prayers from anyone. No hugs, no, I'm thinking of you. I was so angry, I said you know what? I don't want prayer from anybody that's never been there for me. I don't know why I said it because no one was even offering it to me. But once again, I wanted to die. I felt like I failed my son, and no one really cared. They just stabbed me in my heart again and let me live. God showed up and reminded me that he was with me. He sent people that I barely knew or people who knew my son to reach out to me over social media.

I remember there was a community cleanup. I pushed my feelings and went. The chief of police spoke to me and said, unfortunately, I get to see the injustice that's within the system. He said it was a kick in the face to him. A lady officer talked to me out there. She said she watched the video, and everything she saw was him guilty of murder. She knew my son, and she was fighting tears. Then she said an officer is not supposed to cry in their uniform. She asked if I could get another trial or if I could do anything because this just wasn't right. I said no. At that moment, I got the strength to say I will finish this. God give me the strength to write this victim impact statement. I am not a victim. I am a survivor!

After giving them reflections on my son's life and his positive impact on his community, I wrote this. This day, November 18, 2022, I release you, your family, and your friend from hiding you for. I give you no power over my children or my life anymore. This is my prayer. I will always grieve my son, my baby boy, but after today, I will release you to God. That's where my justice lies. The only time I will speak your name is to acknowledge who murdered my son.

What happens for positive change? No amount of time under assault could ever do justice. Nothing could ever undo what you did to my son, his family, friends, or me. Now, you have to live with what you've done for the rest of your life; you've held me captive for two years. I just mourned for two years of my son's murder. Number two of his birthdays. I went without him November 12, his birth, six days later, to look at you, his murderer, once again. But my son wouldn't want me to be held captive like this. He always wanted the best for me and people in general; that's what type of person my son was. So, to live my best possible life of what I have left on this earth, today, I would take steps to process everything fully and properly grieve my son, my baby boy.

Despite it all, my family and I still have the victory. My son left a good legacy at a young age. I am so proud of that, so if you didn't hear anything that I said before, let me say this one more time I am the mother of him, and I release you from my mind and my heart and give you to God. My son's favorite scripture... No Weapon formed against you (which is me) shall prosper.

Now Live, Jeanne, Live.

After I read my speech, I decided that no matter the judge's sentence, I would be OK with it. I never knew that once he said he could only sentence him to the max of 10 years under the second-degree assault, one of the community leaders that was supposed to be supporting me would say that she hoped he appealed that sentence and that the sentence just wasn't correct. This same woman sat on my side of the court the whole week of the trial and came back two months later for sentencing. She sat by my side, and I even thanked her for supporting me. She's a mother herself, a community leader for the youth, and she said this while sitting in the court behind me, his mother, who no longer has her child. It was so unbelievable! I was amazed that she had no remorse or compassion for my mother or my children. If she felt this personally, then why would she be there to support me? Why sit on my side? I felt so many emotions. I felt hurt, betrayed, and angry, but instantly, I started thinking of when my son was first murdered. So, I reached out to a different community leader to see if he would lead a candlelight justice walk for me, and he responded with yes. I felt relieved after that. I waited for him to get back to me with more information. I waited, and I waited. And finally, a friend asked me about the candlelight service. I explained to her that I was waiting on the gentleman to get back to me with more information, so she took it upon herself to reach out to him. She sent me the screenshot of his response.

It read, oh, I get that, but the optics are not good for me to be involved just for that. I think it should be featured more on a mother's loss of all young men, which would gather more support and interest. Are you reading this response? It hurts. I had just lost my son, and all I wanted was a memorial candlelight and walk for him and his life. Now at the time, I needed this just for my son as mothers need individual time first, then it's time to join forces with other mothers. I wasn't worried about the number of people; I wanted to honor my son and bring awareness to violence. I responded back to my friend in a raging anger. I was on fire; I was like a ticking time bomb. I even used some choice curse words. Oh, but as I thought about being hurt by now on two community leaders, this was all just a test.

Through it all, I never gave up. I endured until the end. I did things that I never thought I could do. In the end, that outburst that she had to herself wasn't going to change that day for me. That day remains a day of power and release; that day just revealed the last wolf in the sheep of clothing. In the past 2 1/2 years, things and people have been exposed on this journey. So why would I stay angry, mad, or hurt? They did their jobs, and I'm thankful for being able to see people for who they are. Most importantly, I thank God I listened and did my job until the very end. Whatever else he has for me to do, I will do. I hold no hatred or bitterness towards them when I see them; I can speak and keep it moving. Every test and trial made me who I am today. It doesn't matter who doesn't see me. I finally see myself. My test was for my testimony!

My son's favorite scripture was that no weapon formed against you should prosper. After his death, any time I heard that scripture, it was a bittersweet moment for me. I would think, oh God, why was my son killed with a weapon that was his favorite scripture and then killed with a weapon with one's stab to his heart? A heart that he gave so much love to so many. God let me know his time was up. God allowed this to happen for a reason. There is a greater good in this. And now it's time for Jeanne to live!

When I read those words before the judge, I felt a shift in the atmosphere. The judge stated he never heard a victim impact statement, like mine, in his career as a judge. Since that day, changes came over my life; I realized I had to die to live.

Mother's Love

Born November 12, 1993
God's gift to me
Got trusted me to love guide and teach you
I did just that
The bond we share no one can compare
You are as powerful as thunder, but as gentle as the rain
You brought the sunshine when I had those cloudy days
Once you left my life, it was full of pain
I struggle to suppress my feelings. I was numb.
Days came and days left without no physical or mental rest
Then, one day I felt the sun
I envision your smile
I felt that energy, and I heard your laugh
Some may say I'm crazy, but you never left
The bond we share we share through death
From this pain, I'm feeling I'm finding myself I'm using my voice using loud.
Every day I'm looking for signs while looking up at the clouds
Recharging my energy and getting my rest, I am so thankful for being so blessed
Blessed to be your mother.
Thanking God for choosing me.
I never realized until now
You were here to bless, love, guide and to teach me

I'm growing, using my voice using it loud
Thank you, my son,
From pain to Power
I get it now
My King, My Angel, My Son

JEANNE ELLIOTT

Jeanne Elliott as a loving mother, liturgical, dancer, poet, business owner of Heavenly Hands, LLC, one of the captains of Groove City Girl Trekkers of Cambridge MD. A retired, dialysis technician, CNA, GNA, med tech in medical billing, and coding.

JeanneElliott@ymail.com
FB Heavenly Jean
IG jeanneelliott_7777

The Imposter's Pain is Pain to Grow...Tough From The Womb

By Paula T. Anders

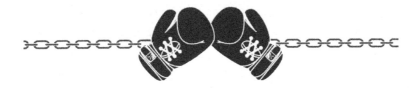

Before becoming a Registered Nurse and ordained Minister of the Gospel, God has always had His hand on me. That's a fact, and as you read, you will understand even more that God has His hands on you, too. You are a winner, and I want you to know WE win whenever we choose God.

One Friday night, in a prayer meeting, I surrendered to the pain of being abandoned, beaten, and humiliated. I cried out to God through my testimony in an all-night shut-in. Oh, Mother Blessinggame, I knew God had sent her to Brown's Temple Church of God in Christ for me. She is this middle-aged woman, short, small-medium built, but she has the strength of eighth Clydesdales Horses carrying a carriage loaded with bricks, and the temperance of a schoolgirl, with a smile of warmth and comfort of pure love and acceptance.

As I think of her acceptance, her warmth fills my heart with joy and eyes with tears because she "Saw Me!" Yes, she saw me and always would say, "God's gotta plan for you, Sister Anders, don't worry, don't fret, and do not look at the people; look to God and hold his word in your heart." She would remind me by saying people, even church people, whom words at times leave you hurt, misunderstood, shattered, to leave you worse than. Those words may have been assigned to hurt you; words disclaimer y'all words do break. Could they pull off the scab of an unresolved issue you haven't healed from? But God, if you aren't afraid to confront the pain, God will give you a word amid your pain.

That's why she told me this, and she encouraged me to always have forgiveness in my heart for those that challenged me and my belief system. You see, what built me is God. He's the source, but he will use, whatever He needs to build you too, and it's found, within the Bible, yes, our instruction book, as a guide for our life. You have to, and I don't like saying you have to, but you have to hide His Holy infallible word in your heart so that you may not sin against God. Help me, Lord God, to always forgive the offenses of others so that I may always be forgiven. Simply forgiving someone is the formula for how we receive forgiveness. If you don't forgive, how can you be forgiven?

If you are having any tinge of awkwardness, then I ask you where or who haven't forgiven. "Create in me a clean heart, O God, and renew a right spirit within me." Psalm 51:10 KJV

"I AM," yes, "I AM," as God said. I am Paula T. Anders, and I can accomplish all things because of my connection to my big brother Jesus, who has already paid the penalty for my sins. So, I can declare with boldness that I am built God tough, for "I AM Paula T. Anders," a woman who survived without knowing her natural father, who survived being abandoned by her adopted father after my mother's death at only sixteen years old.

Now, I have been through some tough stuff, and I am here for it all. I can say that if you surrender to the word of God, not your cousin, sister, friend, or brother, but the Holy Spirit, you can overcome brokenness, torment, abandonment, disgust, failed suicide attempts, depression, dissatisfaction with life, and discontentment. Life can cause you to lose and drift away, but God can help. The same God of Abraham, Isaac, and Jacob is my God, and He has built me tough! God knows your name, and He has built you tough too. Come with me on a journey, and let's discover what's on the other side. You may have tried this or that but allow me to share my journey to wholeness.

I want you to know firsthand, even if you don't want to believe it for yourself, it's easy to believe that you could be walking in the following: Depression, Discontented, and/or Degradation. This will cause you to lose yourself; you are just out here trying to relieve yourself of the pain. Nope, I'm not going to think about those things that will give you a worse feeling; let me just eat something, smoke something, do something, buy something. You become what I know now is a word I've coined this word for myself, "Drifter," and you, if reading this still or know of someone that's comes to mind in this reading. Yes, it becomes too hard to feel; emotions are a catalyst for greater pain, especially if you are getting beaten physically and have already been beaten emotionally with no family support after your mother's death. You are just looking and yearning for someone to "SEE YOU," You never know whom Holy Spirit will use to say something or speak to your spirit, but you will know because it's piercing. Just like when Mother Blessinggame "Saw Me," you want to be seen, heard, and caressed. And when you are homeless, you shut that part of you down because it costs too much to be open with your emotions daily. But as you take this journey to complete wholeness, you too will discover you have to come clean to yourself and hold the mirror to your face to face your face first. Then, I truly believe that as you walk this walk with "I Am," you will discover your strength, your power, and your dexterity to Rise Up and Go Forth in the face of your enemy.

Because I truly believe our God has prepared a table in the presence of our enemy. I, too, didn't even know I was a drifter, but not being rooted and planted, Having been uprooted from the affection of a mother, the normality of a home of day to day knowing you have a home and a home you thought you would always be able to go back to and in an instant an afternoon your life as you dreamt it would be no more. Being homeless did something to my psyche it left me alone with me, and who was I without my room, my childhood home, remember I was sixteen when I became homeless, so yes, the furniture that I picked out, the comforter that spring I had gotten last with my mom. I had wanted my room a dark brown color, and my mom said you would not just have brown, so she allowed me to pick out a chair. It was a rounded carved oak back, and the seat with a soft yellow stripe soft and raised texture. I had a nightstand on which my phone and my romance novels would sit. You know that it was good, I would stay up till three or four AM trying to finish, oh me, the romantic one, I could get lost in those books. It's where I found my peace and truly believed that love was out there and would find me and never let me go. But that's a faint memory because now, where are all those books? Not only my books but my way of life, my home, the smell, my neighbors, my friends, my school, yes, I was in high school, yes, my normal without a mom, without a father, my brother was in only twenty and in the Army and with no loyal family members to extend a helping hand.

You know my mom had three living sisters, I will share with you later in detail; one could cook, and you would eat yourself in a coma. She did not offer a bed, a couch, or even her floor, and she had six children, but when my mom was given her her Dillard Card, I knew this myself because I gave it to her one day she came by when my mom was resting. My mom said to give Aunt Angie that credit card referring to the Dillard card; I overheard their conversation once, and as I recall, it went like this, my mom said, "the girl went used that card, the Dillard card, I'm not going to be able to use it, and I have insurance, so get what you want." Paula brought so much fashion fair makeup that I sent her in there to get foundation because that over-the-counter stuff was not looking good on her skin. She came back with four colors of eyeshadow, blush, two color shadow, eyeliner, lipstick, and some translucent powder. She returned with about two hundred dollars of make-up; I told her she could have still used those Maybelline eyeliner pencils. That's too much money to pay for eyeliner, but the rest, well, she needs it with her skin color; yes, those days were long gone until now. Yes, the journey we are embracing is an out of body experience, yet so many memories are the way of the drift, leaving you with feeling like, where do I belong? My reality was gone, and I had to accept the lot I was given because I couldn't visit that place. It's too painful to the past of uncaring people who only looked out for themselves. But God was there all the time. I thank God for my mom's teachings, like to pray every night, and thank God for waking me every day and for the activities of my limbs.

She never allowed me to feel sorry for myself; she would always remind me that someone has it worse off than you and would be thankful to clean, wash and hang clothes on the clothesline. You know, that's an art, the hanging of the clothes on the clothing lines you see in the south here when I was a child, we had a picnic table, and I would have to pull that reddish bench over to the clothesline to stand so I could reach the clothesline. You would start with the towels and hang them on the back line. You didn't want all the neighbors to the southeast and west of you to know how your underwear was looking. Or how big those panties were, really. There were no thongs back in the day, just briefs, no low riders, or bikini cut, just small, medium, large, and you get my drift. Well, after that, you would hang the rest of the basket, starting with shirts, which took the longest, pants or skirts were easy, and lastly, socks, oh, you could just bunch them up together and be done. Well, being homeless, I would end up either washing at a laundry Matt or using someone's washer/dryer; one of my biggest fears was accidentally breaking it; that is a sure way to get kicked out of someone's home, which allowed you to stay. Well, knowing that you don't belong. I believe this to be true; having gone through many traumatic events and holding or storing the memory within will leave you vague of existence, yet tough for the fight to survive.

As for me, I became a holder of all the pain and abuse I suffered as I pen this chapter, but God, you see, I got saved, I knew God, but I got filled with the Holy Spirit, and baby, that's a new game. When you get filled with the Holy Spirit, you are indeed a new creature. Old things are passed away, and behold, you are anew. You have a new walk, a new talk, a new you. I understand what Mother Blessinggame was telling me, and I'm thankful she came and saw me because on that Friday night prayer, I got my Spiritual Liberty, and yes, who the Son my big brother Jesus Christ did for me on Calvary He set went to hell and got my key to life, and that's life in Christ Jesus. My spirit is alive, and I truly love everybody, and I mean everybody. God's word is a lamp to my feet and a light to my pathway. His word is my breath and my drink. He is everything to this daughter of Zion, and I will bless his Holy Name. Praise the Name of our Risen Savior.

The imposter of pain and pain is you. It's the embodied you; it's not the saved you. It's the memory of you that's been hidden deep to keep the pain or hurt or trauma at bay, not to think on it because it touches a sore place, a place of pain, injury, and or discontentment. And when you come out of the honeymoon of the anointing of the Holy Spirit, then you be able to face the imposter who has been hiding beneath, waiting for her turn to be complete to be recognized to, be acknowledged to be seen fully, not as the drifter the person that has to show up and do everything just right that's part of the anointing of the Holy Spirit trying to get you to trust Him so you will allow Him to lead you into wholeness as He is complete lacking nothing.

"The LORD is my shepherd; I shall not want. He maketh me to lie down in green pastures: He leadeth me beside the still waters. He restoreth my soul: He leadeth me in the paths of righteousness for his name's sake. Yea, though I walk through the valley of the shadow of

death, I will fear no evil: for thou art with me; Thy rod and thy staff comfort me. Thou preparest a table before me in the presence of mine enemies: Thou anointest my head with oil; my cup runneth over. Surely goodness and mercy shall follow me all the days of my life: And I will dwell in the house of the LORD forever."
Psalm 23:1-6 KJV

Just like Jesus, to die is to gain the drifter carried the cross like Jesus carried His cross for you, and I know it's time for you to come, yielding yourself completely to Him, not holding anything back, releasing the pain to Him. This is tough, but He has prepared you now; that is why you are here now. Just like when you felt like everything, school, relationship, solid ones, and finances, you question yourself. I have this; I like to say, "this icky undeserved feeling like I don't need to get so happy or show anyone I'm happy because it will leave it will disappear. To me, I depict it. It's like how Eve and Adam felt after they partook of their forbidden fruit, what just happened, we don't belong here anymore. That's what happened to me, that feeling of drift, after the death of my mom, for forty, yes, forty years. Yet, I want to share this one more tale...

PAULA T. ANDERS

Paula T. Anders is an ordained minister who has a passion for working with singles to encourage them to live a holy and sanctified life of Christ until their soul mate comes along. The name of her ministry is Single Parent Rising, a 501c3 company. Paula believes that her work helps to encourage their hearts because she lives by example as a single parent. Paula is the mother of four children. They are known as the four C's. From eldest to youngest, Chassidy Inez Anders, is the director of tutorial services at University of California, Davis. Collier Paul Anders is an entrepreneur, recently engaged.

Carla Anders is an au pair, and resides presently in Madison, MS, and Cassie Anders is in Nursing School in resides Newport, Arkansas with Paula's only granddaughter Caylee Anders. Now that her children are adults, she still carries that mission. She says, "If I can do it, then you can do it too."

Paula is a minister of the Gospel ordained in 2004 at New Horizon Church International. Where she serves on The Minister's Fellowship Council.

She earned her LPN in 1989 and her RN in 1993.

- The word of God says in Acts 2:44-45 KJV, "44 And all that believed were together, and had all things common; 45 And sold their possessions and goods, and parted them to all men, as every man had need." Paula believes that we are our brothers' keeper, so we should meet the needs of the people. She not only preaches this, but Paula is putting those words into action working with a young woman in need of a safe place to raise her two children after recently having a stroke. The Lord told her to absorb that cost for the ministry. By being obedient to the Lord and supporting people at their lowest, she knew God's in complete control of ministry. Paula believes as a world changer when she can reach one person, and they reach at least one person, then the cycle will continue from person to person, from generation to generation. As an advocate for mental illness, her nursing career spanning over 3.5 decades from delivery of babies to adult, geriatric, and now a focus on mental illness. As a woman and a person who by the Grace of God survived abuse. A dedicated prayer warrior, whose values match her lifestyle. And she believes all things are possible. Every day is the day the Lord made you decide, I simply take the opportunity to stand in the word of God.

He Never Let Me Go
By Betty White Jackson

My whole life has been subject to a God journey. He has proved his strength in, through, and over life my time and time again. I remember laying in my bed, and a song would play over and over again in my mind. Sometimes it would play so loud it would wake me up after I had fallen asleep. I knew that it was God speaking. The song was "Never Let Me Go." "No matter what you're going through, I will never let you go," were the lyrics. Throughout my life, God has always sent little reminders like this to remind me that he is and has been with me from the beginning.

I am the youngest of my siblings. I hear the youngest is the most spoiled in the family. Or gains the most attention. This wasn't true in my case. My mother did not plan on having any more children. As a matter of fact, she took matters into her own hands to make sure that she didn't. After my sister was born, my mom got her tubes tied.

She went to the doctor one day because she wasn't feeling well. The doctor gave her some news. She had a tumor that needed to be treated. Time went on, and the doctor continued treating my mother for a tumor. Only to later find out later that the tumor was me! To her surprise she was pregnant. I was planning, and she was prepared for another child. So, my mother reached out to my aunt and asked her to take me. From birth, my aunt took me in and raised me as her own. It was a typical household. But it was Godless.

We didn't go to church. And I don't remember seeing anyone praying. And I never heard the word "love." Being the only one raised away from my siblings was tough for me. It planted seeds of rejection at an early age. I would often think, "What's wrong with me," or "Why doesn't my mom want me" and "How come no one loves me"? Yes, there were times when I would feel love. But it was something about hearing it. I made a commitment to myself. I said, "When I grow up, I'm going to love hard! And say those words to everybody!" And I did just that. Because of the rejection and love that I didn't feel, I loved with everything in me. But the harder I loved and the more love I gave, the more I felt betrayed by love. Love came back to me as abuse, molestation, and assault.

Is this what love is? I thought. I found myself accepting these forms of love as I continued to search for real love. But I was looking in all of the wrong places. I became a follower of any and everything just to be accepted in my circles of friends. Because I knew that those things weren't really who I was, it never felt natural. Even though I was there, I still didn't feel like I fit in. Even in a room full of people, I still felt lonely. That became me. Always a loaner. But God had a plan for my life even though I didn't see it or even know what a relationship looked like with God. God would always link me with friends who were in church. I remember these friends whose parents were pastors. And in order for me to go play with them, I would have to go to church. I laughed as a child when I would go with them to church. I just thought the people in the church were playing. As I got older, I would finally find friends that I could really connect with, and they would get saved.

I had just given birth to my own child. One of those friends invited me to a see a stage-play called The Rapture. I went and was terrified. I made up my mind that I did not want to be left behind. I decided to get saved. My baby had a severe case of asthma. And I wasn't in the healthiest relationship. I was still on a journey searching for this thing called love but still in all of the wrong places. That same friend told me one day that I had to get out of that bad relationship that I was in. Her exact words were, "You can't be saved and shacking up."

As a babe in Christ, I didn't know how to handle that statement. I was in between really wanting to be saved, but I had no idea how to release myself from a relationship that I was already in before I decided to get saved. It was easy for her to say, come away from the relationship. But as a newbie in salvation, I needed to know how to release myself and walk away. This friend also happened to be my youngest son's babysitter. He had an asthma attack under her care one day. She told me that he had the attack because God was punishing me for staying in that relationship. At that point, I was over it. All I wanted was love and not to be left behind. I didn't want to be punished. I told my friend that I no longer wanted any part of this God. I knew that I was trying my hardest to be the best that I could do in a walk that was new to me. And if you're telling me that I'm being punished for trying, I'm done. So, I never went back to church after that.

I was still on my journey, looking for love. And God was still on a journey to meet me wherever I was. I started a new job. I ran into the most genuine-spirited woman that I have ever met. I continued to watch her daily. I just knew that she was going to change. Everyone else in my life changed me. I was sure that she would too. But she didn't. And she invited me to church over and over again. I would tell her no every time. I meant what I said when I said that I was done and not going back to church. She kept asking. She got me when she invited me to the cookout at church. So, I gathered all of my friends, and we went to the church cookout. We had beer and all the works. I had no regard or respect for God or for church. As time went on, more and more of my friends were getting saved. The Lord kept connecting me with those who would be in the world with me that I really loved and then soon get saved. And because of my hard love for them, I would say, "Well, you hung out with them; you might as well go to church with them." I would visit, but salvation was out.

Then everything in my life took a turn. Things just started going crazy. The rejection and search for love started to get out of control. I was partying every night. If the club closed at 2 am, I went to go find something else that was open. I needed that party adrenaline. I needed to feel something that I didn't feel on a regular. I needed to feel wanted, needed, and loved. Some emotions I just didn't want to feel. So, I would stay out until 4-5 am, get minimal rest, and get up and go to work the next day. This was how I hid. And how I numbed myself. I was numb. But I felt my life as it began to fall apart.

That "fun" life started to become boring to me. Soon I would go out and not even want to dance. Or as soon as I got there, I would be ready to go home. I decided to try this church thing one more time. There was a revival happening. The pastor there called out my name. He said, "You, you."

I went up to the altar. He laid his hands on me and prayed for me. As I walked back to my seat, I felt the spirit of the Lord come over me, and I began to shout and praise God. During this church service, I was by myself and not with my friends. It seemed that God showed up in my darkest hours when I was in those lonely places. He always had to prove to me that He was with me.

I was now saved again, and everything should be fine, right? That's exactly what I thought, or should I say hoped. I just could not get out of this vicious cycle. I could be productive in work and business ventures. But my personal life was still in shambles. The abusive relationship started to overtake me. I knew that I was a good person, and I made a choice for myself. A choice to be happy. In that choice, I decided to take another journey to find it on my own. This journey to find happiness almost resulted in me losing my life. I was still in a relationship that I didn't know how to end. So, I went back to that "one last time." And in this one last time, I truly know that the devil was trying to take my life.

One of the reasons that I went back is because I had gotten ill. And this person said that they would take care of me. And they did. My day of worship came, and I did not want to miss church. I didn't care how sick I was. I remember getting dressed, and he asked, "Where are you getting ready to go"? I said that I was going to church. And he went on to ask me who I was trying to find at church. I said nobody but Jesus. When I said that, the last thing that I remembered was that I was on the floor. I got up, and I just started walking. I was so out of it that I didn't know where I was. I remember seeing water and turning around and seeing him walking behind me. I was so afraid that he was going to throw me into the water. So, I started to pray. I continued to walk. I could barely see. He walked behind me the entire time and didn't say anything. I made it to this restaurant. I asked them to please call the police and the ambulance. I later found out that the impact from the hits gave me a torn retina, a broken nose, and no feeling in the left side of my face.

I remember driving one night, and the Lord spoke to me. "Betty, you have to love yourself as I love you."

In my mind, I said, "I love myself." Then I realized that I was thinking of the outside. I loved my appearance.

But God then said, "You don't love yourself. If you loved yourself, you would not keep running into these bad situations and dealing with these people that are abusing you and taking from you."

From that point on, I started my healing process. I made up in my mind that I was done. And I had to get out of that relationship. I found the strength from God to walk away. The Lord told me that this was my new beginning and that everything that was broken, I had to go back and fix it. I knew that meant the relationship with my mom. I knew that was the seed that planted the rejection, hurt, pain, and trauma. And I did. I asked the Lord to provide a time that I would be able to meet with her alone. She was married at the time, and she and her husband were always together. I reached out to her and asked her if I could stop by. Before this, I couldn't ever tell my mom that I loved her. I was so mad that she gave me away. Because of this, it was also a struggle to trust people. And I would only let people get only so close to me. I finally sat down with her. I asked her one question. Little did I know that every burden and shackle would fall off of me from asking that one question. My healing wasn't in her answer. It didn't matter what her answer was. Whatever was ok with me. My healing came in, releasing the question.

"Why did you give me away," I asked. She started talking. I still don't know what she said. I was so focused on the freedom that I felt at that moment. All of my life, I had that question inside of me, around me, and over me. From that point on, I felt so free. I could see it again. The grim of smoke wasn't around me anymore. I didn't feel heavy anymore. After all of this time, I finally found the love and happiness that I was searching for. It was in my freedom. I was able to show and accept love from my mother. And in that moment, I knew that God had never let me go, no matter what I was going through.

BETTY WHITE JACKSON

Betty **White Jackson** is a licensed insurance / final expense specialist and a strong advocate for youth and adolescents. Betty is a native of Salisbury and has worked in the nonprofit community in Salisbury and surrounding areas for the last 20 years. She received a Master's Degree in Social Work from Salisbury State University with a focus on community organization and change. Betty has a strong sense of devotion to empowering, promoting, and improving the quality of life for the better good of the community. Betty is the mother of two sons, Kevin and Gary. In her downtime, she enjoys reading, listening to music, and going to the gym. She loves to travel, and she loves to eat. Serving God and spending time with her family and friends is a top priority for her.

Survivor No, Overcomer, Yes!

By Shashawna Johnson

Originally when I was asked to be a part of this amazing project, I was overjoyed and truly blessed by the invitation. As time went on, I began to feel overwhelmed and doubtful. I asked myself, "Shawna, why did you really say yes? You aren't properly positioned to be a part of this book. You are lacking in so many areas, and you are not worthy. Who could your testimony possibly help?"

There was even a time I typed out a whole message to Tamyra saying that I apologize for wasting her time, but I can't do this, and I think I made a mistake by accepting. Knowing my sister in Christ, I already knew that she wasn't having that. So, I deleted the text, and honestly, I continued to procrastinate. I kept thinking about all the things the Lord has brought me through, all the things he covered me from, and I kept saying I just don't know what to talk about. At least, that's what I kept telling myself. All along, I knew two things. One, I knew that it was only the enemy trying to deter me from sharing a piece of my testimony and two, I knew exactly what I was supposed to share.

I was raised in the church, but of course, like so many others, when I got older, I strayed away and did my own thing in the world. Let me tell you it took a bad situation to bring me back to God. He had to touch the one thing I held in higher regard than him, my child. That is a different testimony for a different time. I said that to say I remember when I came back to church, and I gave my Yes. The enemy bombarded my mind with so many doubts and negative thoughts about myself, making me want to give up. In this case, I would soon discover it was history repeating itself. One morning I woke up out of a dead sleep and said, "That's what is happening."

I realized at that moment that I gave my Yes for this project. The enemy's goal was to try to discourage me from sharing. That's when I knew that I had to move forward, and yet I still drug my feet up until the last minute.

A week or so went by, and I continued to wrestle with what I was going to share. I knew that I needed to share about the loss of my sister because it was the one moment in my life when I felt completely broken and at my lowest. Out of everything I have been through, including the loss of my father, the loss of my sister was too much for me to handle. The Lord let me know through this process of sharing that I would receive my complete healing from the situation. I know it may seem crazy to some, but in a way, I did not want to receive my true healing. I felt like it was almost a betrayal not to carry this hurt and this pain around with me. Almost as if I wasn't hurting, and I was too happy that I was forgetting about her in some way. The enemy tried to convince me that I was bound to this depression forever, but the devil is a liar! So, come with me on this journey of healing as I share my testimony. I hope that it Blesses you as it sets me free.

On Thanksgiving Day, 2020, while eating dinner with close friends, I found out about my grandmother's passing. Of course, I was naturally sad; even though it was expected, and she lived a full life, it was still painful. Especially watching my mother, aunts, and uncle deal with the loss of their mother. Unfortunately, I knew the feeling all too well, having lost my own father back in 2018. It was tough for me. My dad was my best friend; I could literally talk to him about anything. He was my rock and often gave me honest, Godly advice. I didn't feel like I could do life without him. Losing him was what I thought was the hardest moment of my life. A few years later, I would learn it indeed would not be.

Shortly after my grandmother's passing, my baby brother and my sister were both admitted to the hospital in December of the same year. My baby brother contracted Covid-19, and my sister suffered from a mild stroke. My baby brother was not doing well when he was admitted because he suffered from severe asthma and was immediately placed on a ventilator and was unresponsive. Surprisingly, my sister was doing well. We talked every single day. I even joked about breaking her out of the hospital if they did not release her before Christmas. Sadly, my baby brother passed on December 27, 2020, from complications with Covid-19. His funeral was on January 2, 2021. After getting back in town from the funeral, I was mentally, emotionally, and physically exhausted. All I wanted to do was get some rest and try to wrap my mind around the loss of two of my immediate family members in such a short amount of time. I just wanted to calm my spirit; regretfully, that little peace of mind I tried to acquire would not last long.

The day after the funeral, I slept in. A pounding on my front door awakened me. It actually scared me. The knocking was so loud. I got up and answered the door to my oldest brother, who told me they had been trying to call me. He said I needed to hurry and get dressed, that we had to get to the hospital because something was going on with my sister. I got dressed, and we all went up to the hospital. They explained to us that my sister had now suffered two significant back-to-back strokes, that her brain had completely shifted to one side of her skull, that the damage was irreversible, that she was entirely brain dead, and that she would never recover. They wanted us to make the decision whether or not to take her off of life support.

At that moment, it felt like all the breath had left my body. I felt like I was on the outside, watching everyone's reaction, including my own. I just thought it's no way that this could be real. We just laid my baby brother to rest yesterday.

We left the decision to take her off of life support to her to her husband, and that's what was decided. In days to come, I felt an array of emotions. Of course, sadness, disbelief, and so much anger. I was angry with God; I felt like he let me down not only in this instance but also with my dad and brother. I was mad at myself. I remember praying profusely for my dad, my baby brother, and my sister. I thought I had the gift of healing; why isn't it working for them? Why would he allow me to be a vessel of healing for others but not for my own family members? I felt betrayed. I know it is selfish, but I was angry because God heard the prayers of others that were going through the exact times with their families. I questioned why he did not honor my prayers. I started to doubt everything; I felt like, in some way, it was my fault (I should have prayed harder and fasted longer).

Weeks following my sister's funeral, I lost all interest in going to church. I tried everything in my power to numb the pain. For the most part, I hid how I was truly feeling from everyone. Of course, everyone knew I was sad, but I don't think they truly realized the gravity of the situation. I just went on with trying to be there for everyone else. Trying to be strong for my mom, brothers, nieces and nephews, and children, all while I was dying inside. I felt like I needed to be the "Strong One." My sister and I argued a lot, but she was always my greatest support system. We could argue one day, and the next, if I needed it, she would give me the shirt off her back.

She wasn't only my greatest support system; she was a great sister, and aunt to her nephews. She was my protector. Everyone knew not to mess with Shette's little sister. LOL. My birthday was three days before hers, but we were two years apart; she was older. I was actually supposed to be born on her birthday. For almost 35 years, we shared and celebrated our birthdays together. Even if I decided to go on vacation, we would always celebrate together when I got back. So, what would I do now with our birthday coming up? I felt like I was robbed of my closest, oldest friend. I felt like she didn't get to live her life, and it shouldn't have been cut short because there was so much more she was destined to do. Who would I pick on and argue with? Why her? Why not me?

Depression overtook me. I fell back into smoking marijuana, drinking heavily, and cutting off communication with those I knew could help me. I was just out here doing the most. Trying to ease the pain. Trying to prove to God that I did not need him; I could do it all alone because he wasn't dependable. One night, I remember driving drunk on a back road, and a deer hopped out in front of the car. We were literally about an inch from hitting it. It stood in the middle of the road perfectly still, and we looked at each other, then it just ran off into a field. I was working a job where they did random drug tests, yet I was never selected, while every other single person working in my office was. One day, I started to feel horrible; I went to work and ended up having to be rushed to the hospital from work. Come to find out; I had a sepsis infection in my blood that was shutting down my organs.

While in the hospital while surrounded by loved ones, I had never felt so lonely. They told me that if I had not made it to the hospital in time, I would have likely been dead by that night. I felt like I was dying. My body was wracked with pain, I had a fever that they could not break, my heart was shutting down, and they had me on a heart monitor. At that point, I began to make my peace with God. I said Lord, I know it's my time to go, and I know that these last two years I have lived in sin and denied you in any way possible, but please, Lord, forgive me. I prayed for my children, mom, and brother that God be their strength. Through tears, I began to recite the Lord's prayer, and, in the mist, I heard him say daughter, this isn't your time. I began to weep heavily and say, Lord, after all, I have done, I deserve to die, but I continued to pray.

In my prayer, he brought things to my remembrance; when you almost hit the deer daughter, it was me who blocked it. When your job was doing random drug screens, I hid your name. When you sat on the edge of your bed and contemplated suicide, it was me who made you think about your children and what they would do without you. When you were so intoxicated you did not even know how you made it home, I showed you traveling mercies. When you were getting high and decided to listen to your worship music and went into your Heavenly tongues while under the influence. It was me trying to show you that you are never too far gone. And at this moment, you humbly submitted yourself unto me; I will heal your body. For almost two weeks, I sat in the hospital and never even reached out to my leadership. Even though I lived in direct sin for two years, my leadership never stopped reaching out, checking on me, encouraging, me, and sending their love. After praying, I then reached out to my headship to share with him what the Lord revealed to me in prayer.

The Lord told me that my testimony would help set those grieving free. He showed me my future self, sharing my testimony, his word, and even back to ministering in dance. I just did not understand how this would come to pass. It is so crazy because before I started writing, I forgot that God had already spoken this into existence. Wow, my mind is truly blown at this very moment. Continuing, I shared this and some other things with my leadership. Y'all God never took his hands off me. He has been with me through this entire journey. Even when I turned my back on him and shunned him, HE LOVED ME! He showed me, Mercy and Grace. He kept me when I deserved nothing but death. Our best is only filthy rags to him, and I was giving him my worst, and he did not give up on me. You are never too far gone to come back to God! He Loves all of us. Psalm 86:15, "But you, O Lord, are a God of compassion and mercy, slow to get angry and filled with unfailing love and faithfulness." You were faithful to me God! Hallelujah! I am not a survivor; I AM AN OVERCOMER through the strength and love of God....

Please, if you take anything from my testimony. Remember, the enemy is cunning, but he is ultimately a liar. Remember, God loves you, and he will never give up on you. It is we who give up on ourselves. You may not understand a lot of things but trust God anyway. When you are in turmoil, seek him even more and draw closer to him. I pray that this blesses someone and thank you for this opportunity. Shawna out!

SHASHAWNA JOHNSON

Who is **Shashawna Johnson**? She is a mother, a daughter, a sister, and a friend, but most importantly, she is a daughter of the most high, and a woman of God. Kind, loving, nurturing, bold, courageous, and strong. Overall, a survivor. A survivor of domestic abuse, a survivor of divorce, a survivor of death, a survivor of great loss, a survivor of severe depression, and suicidal thoughts, all through the Grace of God. I remember years ago walking into my leadership's office with an outline of a program I wanted to start for young women facing all types of adversity. Young Woman Opposing Compromise, that was the first time I felt that I had purpose in the Kingdom of God. Desiring to be used, I submitted myself and was imparted with the gift of Healing. Humbly being a vessel, used at the Lord's will, even while facing my own adversities. Now I realize I'm more than a survivor; I'm an Overcomer!!!!

Contact: Shashawna Johnson
Email: srjohnson1011@gmail.com

Can't Kill Purpose; Just Hold On

By Dorothea Cephas

A mother will always protect and be a covering for their children. However, circumstances will arise in your baby, child, teen, or young adult lives that a parent can't help—for example, things such as cancer or losing a child to a car accident. A mother watching her firstborn and only biological daughter give birth to two stillborn babies what an indescribable feeling. Imagine receiving a phone call saying, Are you the mother of Ms. Jackson? We have Ms. Jackson in the maternity ward, and the baby is deceased. My response was, "I'm on my way." Immediately when I arrived, seeing my daughter in labor and delivery, knowing that she would not be bringing a baby home, was heart-wrenching.

The medical team was extremely empathic and answered all questions. In my mind, I was praying to God, asking for a Lazarus experience. I believed God for a miracle. I was thinking that once she gives birth to the baby, the baby girl will start to cry, and we will be able to rejoice. There's always hope, right? As my only biological daughter had to go through the process about 30 minutes before giving birth, her body went into shock, and her body started shaking uncontrollably. The nurses and doctor immediately came into the labor and delivery room. The charge nurse looked me dead in my eyes while lying across my daughter, doing all she could do to care for my daughter. With tears in her eyes, she said, "We lost your grand baby; we won't lose your daughter."

The medical team wrapped my daughter up in plastic; now I know it was the type of compression to get her blood circulating. The medical team was phenomenal! My daughter eventually came around.

I still believe in God for a miracle. My daughter had her biological father, stepfather, maternal grandmother, and myself all in the room with her. No one knew I was still praying and believing God for this miracle as my daughter went through the birthing process of pushing my granddaughter out. The room was completely silent; no crying, no congratulations, no nothing.

The nurse wrapped and cleaned my deceased grand baby off and gave the baby to my daughter. The dr pulled the family aside and showed us the afterbirth in the umbilical cord, there was a blot clot—the blood clot cut off my granddaughter's air supply. The doctor stated that she wasn't supposed to show us, however; she felt the need to in order for my daughter to grieve properly. My daughter's body was developing blood clots, and there was a clot in the umbilical cord that cut the baby's air supply off. After comforting my daughter, I stepped out of the room, questioning God, why didn't you grant me this miracle? I looked down the hall and saw that the nurse was in tears. The nurse came over to me and said "I'm so sorry."

After the emotional experience with the nurse, I called on my late pastor Martha T. Smith. I explained to her what happened. In my pastor's sickness, she got her husband to bring her to see my only daughter. After 24 hours, my daughter was discharged and had to plan a home-going service. I wrote an obituary for my granddaughter. That doesn't even set right in my soul. We planned a beautiful service for my first granddaughter. I didn't show any emotion until we went to a gravesite. That's when I had to accept the fact that the Lazarus moment wouldn't happen for us. I don't want to be "Built God Tough" I'm tired of one thing after another. Just tired!

After about two years or so, my daughter gave birth to my second-born granddaughter, "India Star" My daughter had a high-risk pregnancy; thank God India made it! About three years after India, my daughter married and gave birth to my first grandson. My grandson was born dead for 8 minutes. Dead on arrival. I was at work. I was approximately one hour and 25 minutes from my daughter. I called my cousin, who lived about 5 minutes from the hospital where my daughter was. By the time my cousin got to the hospital, my daughter was prepared for surgery. This particular hospital had no medical records on my daughter. The doctor stated that my grandson's heartbeat was dropping rapidly, and if she didn't get him out quickly, we would lose him. The doctor asked my daughter, "Do you give me permission to perform surgery?"

My daughter shook her head "Yes," and at the time, all the information that particular hospital had on my daughter was her name and birthrate.

The doctor said, "Miss, I wasn't supposed to resuscitate for eight minutes. I was supposed to stop after four–five minutes. Did God just give me the Lazarus experience? Now somebody say, "Glory!" My grandson was on life support and my daughter was stable. After an hour, my grandson was flown to children's hospital in Washington, DC, the number one hospital dealing with premature babies in The United States of America.

My grandson is currently thriving and doing well. Approximately two years after my grandson, my daughter had another stillborn birth. Lord, this is too much; I am thankful for my first grandson's life; however, not again. I went to the hospital where my daughter was and comforted her. My daughter had rung the bell to get the nurse to help her use the bathroom. My daughter started screaming and yelling that the baby was coming out. I was questioning God and actually exhausted without showing it. My daughter looked at me and said, "Thank you, mom for raising us in church because I wouldn't have known how I would have made it without God and my faith."

As I questioned God, my daughter was thankful for the strength and knowledge to know that God gets the glory in it all. Reality check! Talking about being "Built God Tough."

Imagine working for an agency for 20 years and getting terminated prior to termination. Never had a write-up, had the keys to unlock the building, had all access codes, trained staff and ran two centers at a time. Yes, that happened to little ole me. The leadership of this particular agency changed. It was one thing that quickly became Political Supporters, and I watched how this particular agency got rid of every person of color over nothing. I was the longest and last person of color in this specific office space.

During the pandemic, I went into the office at least four days a week to service families. All the time, effort, and dedication meant nothing; people will bless and curse you with the same tongue. A few things transpired via email, and I responded, however, when I responded, my response went to every person in the agency. My response was factual evidence. I was locked out of the company email and asked to come in two days later. I knew I was getting terminated by how they did others. Imagine me in a board room with an "Uncle Tom," and the rest don't look like me.

"The result is that we will have to let you go, and you can make an appointment to get your things out of the office." They said. I looked at the devil in their eyes and asked whether I would be eligible for unemployment. They verbally said, "Yes."

Then I said, "I'm here now. One of you can walk me over to get all of my things right now." I was terminated in November 2020 with no money, unemployment, or anything. My sisterhood circle didn't let me fall. I was receiving cash apps and pushing my jewelry sales. I didn't even factor in what if I get the COVID-19 virus. No job, no unemployment; my daughter and myself ended up being hospitalized, fighting for our lives in two separate hospitals. Imagine being on your deathbed, and your daughter is on hers, suffering from the same thing. In a worst-case scenario, my oldest son had to make all medical decisions for us. Every time I got strength, I called about my daughter.

All I could do was look at her via face time. I could barely talk or breathe. After one day, God spoke to me and said "you can't kill purpose." Then I knew I was going to make it out. God granted me a Lazarus experience! Good God almighty from Zion! Imagine no visitors. You're sick and trying to comprehend your health while deeply concerned about your firstborn child. God brought us both out. We are warriors! We are chosen by God. I get asked all the time, "You must have a man. You're so happy."

I laugh and say, "I'm *single.*"

I'm happy because I am healed; I'm happy because I truly thank God for life. I have my life, and all of my children are above ground. I don't have money, I'm living paycheck to paycheck like a lot of Americans; I don't have a fancy house or car. BABY! I have a life! I'm happy to be able to smell, eat, breathe, see, and touch; I have a place to live and a car to drive. It's the small things that make me happy. I'm happy to have love and joy. My God is everything, and he Built and designed me to be "Built God Tough." Remember, you are the head and not the tail. You are above and not beneath. You're the lender and not the borrower in Jesus's name. The only thing stopping you is you. Keep going and look up.

DOROTHEA CEPHAS

Dorothea Cephas is a single mother of 4 and a grandmother. Dorothea is an Encourager, Family Advocate, and Bestselling Co-Author of The Women of Influence Anthology. Dorothea has her bachelor's degree in Applied Behavioral Science. Dorothea has worked with families and children for over 20 years. Dorothea has been a character count coach teaching youth about the six pillars of character trustworthiness, respect, responsibility, fairness, caring, and citizenship. Dorothea is passionate about her Building Kings & Queens platform, where she can uplift and encourage the youth of today. Dorothea Cephas stands firm on the word of God; she makes everyone around her smile and sees the positive in all things. Dorothea children mean the world to her they are her heartbeat. Dorothea would give up her life for her children and grandchildren. Dorothea advocates for the youth in her community. Dorothea is ambitious, determined, and loyal. Dorothea goes by Queen Cephas; Dorothea's motto is "Keep pushing! Keep pressing!"

Dorothea can be reached on all social media platforms.
Facebook: Dorothea Cephas
IG: queencephas1
Tiktok: queencephas
Email: oneofakindjewels4@gmail.com

God Tough
(Official Song Lyrics)
By Tee Hubbs

Hook:
Build me up
I ain't breaking
I'm God tough
I ain't shaking
Build me up
I ain't breaking
I'm God tough
I ain't shaking

Verse 1:
Big body build,
taking whatever you throwing.
These demons and seeing me,
they ain't got nothing for me.
Riding on prayer,
High off life
Now I'm growing.
I'm turning down my plate,

that's how I gain momentum.
Father, son, Holy Ghost, yeh
That's a Triple turbo
Top speed cause my God,
you know he official
I'm built not to break but to last through this mission.
Got my bass pro hat on cause I'm going fishing.
Take a seat and just listen.
I was rough around the edges
Went from 0-100 real quick
Now resistant.
Built on a firm foundation.
Now I'm sturdy and conditioned.
Tried by the fire. Yup.
Devil you a liar.
Red-blooded bought
Powerful, unbreakable.
Tough as nails, unshakable.
The rugged cross saved me boi
On the rough side of the mountain.
You can find me music blasting
Trying to make it in.
Built me bad with tough skin.
took my mind, gave me his
Took my hand, married me
Turned me around, I back slid.
Now I'm back, focused
When I'm weak, he strengthened
Tougher, tougher than your average.
So salute.

Yea. I'm built for this.

Hook:
Build me up
I ain't breaking
I'm God tough
I ain't shaking
Build me up
I ain't breaking
I'm God tough
I ain't shaking

Verse 2:
Tryna be hard but he tougher than your whole crew.
Why don't you surrender cause he's got some bigger
plans for you.
Go hard in the paint,
It's shades of red everywhere.
Then it turn to white,
He got up on the third day.
He building his church on the solid rock I stand.
Ain't nothing stronger the man who hung by his
hands.
If I were you, I would move expeditiously.
Call me Joe Clark I learned how to lean on him.
I'm built God Tough
He the one who charge me up.
I was lost for a while
But thank God I found the plug.

Outro:
Build me up
I'm God Tough
Build me up
Build me up
Built God Tough.

Watch official music video here:
https://youtu.be/f0BxQZtMO2s

Made in the USA
Middletown, DE
14 October 2023

40769021R00170